GULF STATES

J·P·M
PUBLICATIONS

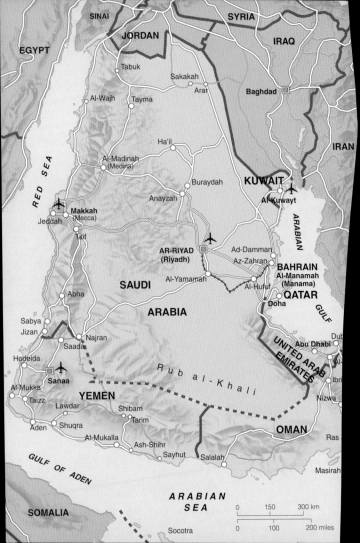

CONTENTS

KUWAIT

Resolutely Modern

Behind its improbable landmark of a trio of public-utility towers, Kuwait City is a gleaming capital of highrises, hugging the shores of the upper Arabian Peninsula. Among the modern palaces, cavernous mosques, shiny shopping malls and office buildings, you may perceive remnants of old city ramparts and walled-in residences tucked away in corners of urban development. A web of six- and eight-lane motorways fans out from the capital, sometimes as jam-packed with traffic as the expressways of Los Angeles. The scars left by the Gulf War have almost healed, and the country is largely back to its old self.

Bordered by Iraq, Saudi Arabia and the turquoise waters of the Gulf along its eastern coastline, Kuwait is even smaller than Wales. Its 17,800 sq km (6,880 sq miles) are mostly desert, a sprawling, empty expanse with only a tiny settlement of black Bedouin tents here and there on a faraway horizon. Until the discovery of oil, fishing and pearl diving were the principal occupations, which long ago strengthened the region's trading prominence and put it on the map as an important transit point for merchants voyaging between Asia and Europe. Nowadays, oil provides most of Kuwait's income; the Burgan oil fields are the world's second largest after those of Saudi Arabia. Over 2 million barrels of black gold are pumped every day, now that the massive mopping-up operations of the early 1990s are completed.

The National Assembly represents the only elected parliament of all the Gulf States, while the Emir of Kuwait heads a dynasty that traces its origins to 1753. To keep the country humming, a huge foreign workforce is necessary: of the estimated 1.8 million inhabitants of the Emirate, less than half are Kuwaiti.

A Brief History

2000 BC	Failaka, the largest of the country's nine islands, is a trading station and possibly an outpost of the fabled Bahrain-based Dilmun civilization.
4th century BC	Under Alexander the Great, the Greeks settle on Failaka and call it Ikaros. It becomes a fishing and pearling centre.

17th century AD	Around 1672, the ruler of the Bani Khalid tribe, Barrak bin Ghurian, builds a *kut*, a small house constructed like a fortress, on the mainland. (It is thought that the name Kuwait derives from *kut*).
18th–19th centuries	Several tribes migrate to the area, among them the Bani Utubi, comprised of several subgroups including the Al-Sabah, Al-Khalifa and Al-Zayed families. Ending a period of tumultuous rivalry, Sheik Sabah bin Jaber is unanimously chosen around 1753 to administer justice and handle affairs of state. The Ottomans try to absorb Kuwait into their empire, without success. Sheik Mubarak signs an agreement with Britain in 1899, by which, in exchange for the Royal Navy's protection, he gives Britain responsibility for the country's foreign affairs.
20th century	In the 1920s, the *ikhwan* brotherhood led by Abdul Aziz Al-Saud attempts to incorporate Kuwait, and a defensive wall is quickly built around Kuwait City. Britain relinquishes its rights in 1961 and the country becomes independent. Oil revenues increase in the 60s and 70s and a high standard of living is achieved.
	Kuwait is attacked and overrun by Iraqi forces on 2 August, 1990, obliging the ruling family to flee across the border to Saudi Arabia. A few weeks later, Iraq declares Kuwait its 19th province, prompting a U.S.-led international coalition force to conduct six-week air and ground attacks to rout the occupier and liberate the country on 27 February, 1991.

Kuwait City

In the heart of Kuwait City, the uninspiring main street, Fahd al-Salem, is bordered by cheap shops and modest glass and steel office buildings which sprouted in a hurry after the oil boom of the 1970s. Remains of one of the city's five gates from the 1920 walls sit on top of a roundabout mound at the foot of the boulevard.

The Arabian Gulf Road follows the coastline for miles around the bays before angling southwards. The large white edifice with sloping roof is the **National Assembly Building**, badly damaged during the Gulf War but now restored, and the meeting place of the Gulf's only elected parliament. It was designed by Jørn Utzon, of Sydney Opera House fame. Offshore you can see the ship that 7 once served as the luxury Al-Salem Hotel, permanently moored here but completely burned out by the Iraqis in 1990–91.

The **National Museum**, once a priceless showcase of Islamic art, now stands grimly empty as a reminder of the looting and vandalism of the Gulf War. Part of the building is being restored to display whatever the government can manage to gather together.

Nearby, the tumbledown **Sadu House**, a century old, contains a collection of Bedouin women's woven goods. Next door is the spacious **Al-Bader House**, built between 1838 and 1848, with fine examples of old carved wooden doors, thatched ceilings, stables, modest-sized living quarters but wide courtyards.

To get an idea of what the old settlement of Kuwait would have looked like, a **replica town** has been set up, where children like to play but also serving for traditional cultural events. Nearby in the **dhow harbour,** scores of teakwood vessels anchored together await sunset, when they head out to sea for a night of fishing. Other traditional boats are used for transport.

Sief Palace is the seat of the Emir's court, where his day-to-day business is carried out. Opposite is the truly **Grand Mosque**, built in 1986 at a cost of nearly $40 million to accommodate 10,000 worshippers.

Designed by Swedish architects, the **Kuwait Towers** on the headland are visible from every direction. The pair on the coast are intended for the city's water storage. The highest globe, at a height of 122 m (400 ft), is a revolving observation deck, offering a breathtaking panoramic view over the Gulf and environs of Kuwait City. The lower globe, at 88 m (289 ft), contains a restaurant. The nearby spike tower handles the city's electricity requirements and lights up the other two. But the highest peak on the skyline is the Telecommunications, or **Liberation Tower**, at 370 m (1,214 ft), in the centre of town. Its revolving viewing platform gives a lookout point almost 30 m (100 ft) higher than that of the water towers.

Beneath the Kuwait Towers is **Aqua Park**, providing hours of entertainment with swimming pools, winding water chutes, lazy river and beach.

A mile or so down the Arabian Gulf Road, tiny **Green Island** is connected by a pedestrian causeway. A pavement train takes passengers around the isle to a photo-opportunity spot to capture the Kuwait Towers on film.

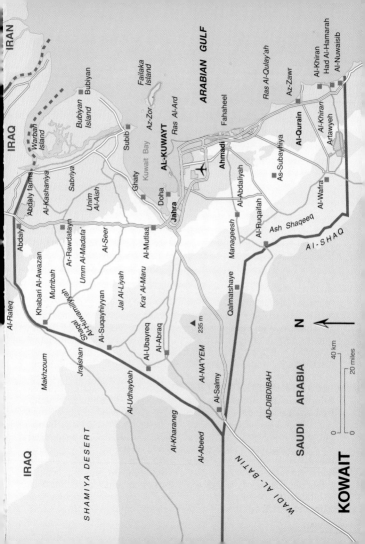

Scale model of a dhow is admired by one and all.

A drive south along the Arabian Gulf Road takes you past rambling palaces and residences to **Salmiya**, a favourite town with Kuwait's young crowd because of its fast-food and retail outlets. The remarkable Pyramid Mosque, perhaps unique in the Islamic world, is strangely sited on one of the town's major roundabouts.

In the Jabriya district to the west of Salmiya, the **Tariq Rajab Museum**, housed in the basement of a villa, contains a dazzling private collection of Islamic art, folk jewellery, ceramics, manuscripts, calligraphy, musical instruments, metalware and costumes—some many centuries old. Tastefully organized exhibits span Central Asian and Middle Eastern cultures.

Towards the Desert

In the last days of the 1990–91 occupation, a corps of resistance fighters held off against Iraqi forces from villas in **Al-Qurain**, south of Kuwait City. The two houses, preserved as a **martyrs' museum**, have been left in the state in which the allied forces found them: bullet-ridden, shelled by a tank, vandalized, with blood-splattered walls and floors where resistance fighters were slain—a moving reminder of the Gulf War.

In the Bedouin town of **Jahra**, west of Kuwait City, is the **Red Fort**, or Palace. The spacious 19th-century fortress, actually sand-coloured, was the scene of important battles including Kuwait's struggle for independence from the Saudis in 1920.

Ahmadi is the heart of Kuwait's Burgan oil fields. The Kuwait Oil Company's Petroleum Display Centre has exhibits on oil production, drilling and pumping processes, and also shows how the company tackled the problems of environmentally devastating burning oil fields and oil lakes left in the wake of the Gulf War.

For something more lighthearted, **Entertainment City**— about 20 km (12 miles) northwest of Kuwait City—provides for a relaxing day with theme parks, fountains and lakes, funfair rides and recreational activities. Just outside Entertainment City is Kuwait's major dhow-building yard where with a bit of luck you'll see a traditional teakwood vessel under construction.

Eating Out

Most of Kuwait's fine dining rooms are in the hotels, but across the country you'll discover Arabic, Asian and European restaurants—not to mention a proliferation of American fast-food eateries. However, this is the place to indulge in Indian food, for you will find everything from samosa stalls to comfortable restaurants serving delicious food from every region of India. The Kuwaitis adore buffets, where they can sample a bit of everything. You can order a serving of appetizers *(mezze)* which are often enough to make a filling meal on their own.

Kebabs, rice casseroles, lamb baked whole and honey-soaked sweets—usually from traditional Levantine cookery—are sure to be on offer.

Shopping

Here you can choose between glitzy malls and open-stall bazaars, selling everything from pigeons and pulses to sandals and spices.

The chic Salhiya complex, an enormous annex to the Méridien Hotel, houses the country's finest shops with luxury goods from around the world. But Al-Khaleejia, Al-Muthanna and a dozen other shopping centres in Kuwait offer wide ranges of merchandise, too.

In quarters both creakingly old and spanking new, it's a pleasure to amble through the markets with their stalls of fresh produce, the glittering gold souk and the bazaar where Bedouin women sell both traditional and more contemporary household wares. Jewellery and textiles are competitively priced, and you'll soon pick up haggling skills as you go along. In the gold 11 souk, the precious metal is sold at 18–22 carats in Arabic and Indian heavyweight styles or in more delicate European designs.

Wander through the *souk hareem* (women's souk), the Abbasiya souk (where goods are both bought and sold), and the souk Al-Jouma (the name means Friday Market, but it's also open Wednesdays and Thursdays), where treasure hunters will find carpets, rugs, old brass and copperware in a flea-market ambiance.

Practical Information

Clothing. Wear light, airy cottons when out and about, shopping, touring, etc. But if dining in an elegant restaurant, you might choose to dress up a bit in air-conditioned comfort. Don't forget that you're in an Islamic country and are asked to respect local customs: women shouldn't wear mini-skirts and men should avoid wearing shorts in the street. On the beach or at the swimming pool, the usual bathing suit is fine though topless is definitely not acceptable.

Currency. The dinar, abbreviated KD, is divided into 1,000 fils: 1 KD = 1,000 fils. Notes: 250 and 500 fils; KD 1 to 20. Coins: 5 to 100 fils. Rates are generally better in currency-exchange offices than at hotels.

Hours. Shops are usually open 8.30 a.m.–12.30 p.m., closing for a long siesta, then re-opening from 4.30 to 9 p.m. Government offices are open Saturday to Wednesday 7.30 a.m.–1.30 p.m., Thursday 7.30–11.30 a.m.; in summer, hours move back 30 min. The local weekend is Thursday and Friday.

Language. Arabic is the national language though English is widely understood.

Photography. To avoid any unpleasantness, ask permission before taking photos of the Kuwaitis—particularly women who tend to be camera-shy.

Religion. Islam is the official religion though Christian denominations (Anglican, Reformed, Roman Catholic) also have churches in Kuwait. During the fasting month of Ramadan, visitors must respect local custom by not eating, drinking or smoking in public during the day. Once the sun sets, the abstinence is over until sunup next day. International hotels have a daytime dining room for non-Muslims.

BAHRAIN

Desert Island

For some, it was the biblical Garden of Eden. For others, it was the paradise that the ancients sang praises to as the Land of the Living or the Land of the Rising Sun. Bahrain is the Dilmun of the epic of Gilgamesh, an ancient Sumarian text written 4,000 years ago. The Dilmun civilization was flourishing while the rest of the world was emerging from the last stages of the Ice Age.

The desert isle—Bahrain Island is actually the biggest of a group of more than 30 islands—is a veritable treasure trove of remnants of this proud era: from tens of thousands of burial mounds and temples to foundations of forts and an entire 4,000-year-old village. Tucked in the emerald waters of the Arabian Gulf between Qatar and Saudi Arabia, Bahrain became a key commercial centre in ages past for the people of the region. Merchants from Greece, Mesopotamia and Sumeria to the north came to Bahrain to haggle over goods with traders from India, Oman and the eastern African coasts to the south. Gold, pearls, spices and valuable hand-crafted wares were among coveted items brought to Bahrain. The island gained an enviable position in Arabia for its fresh water and for the remarkable quality of its pearls, called "fish eyes" in ancient writings.

Among the peoples who scrapped over Bahrain or tried to dominate it were Sumerians, Persians, Greeks, Bedouins, Portuguese and Turks. At the end of the 18th century, Ahmed al-Fatih conquered the island and established the Al-Khalifa dynasty which continues to rule over the State of Bahrain today. The present population of 550,000 is mainly concentrated in the northern third of the island, which is only 50 km long and 16 km wide (30 miles by 10). A third of the population is foreign, mainly hailing from Asia, but there are also those from other Arab countries and expats from the West, most of whom have come here to work.

Like a mirage, dozens of gleaming office buildings and luxury hotels dominate the skyline of Manama, the capital. Most of these modern edifices were constructed on land reclaimed from the sea. The surface area was increased by one-fifth thanks to land reclamation—and it's still growing. In the face of dwindling oil reserves, the nation set itself on a course of industrial diversification which includes aluminium plants as well as shipbuilding and repair yards. Without seriously altering the old quarter of Manama, the new lands have helped make Bahrain an important banking and commercial centre in the region.

But visitors wanting to escape from towering glass and steel have only to stroll a few metres to older districts. In modern Bahrain, the past is never very far away. Venerable residences, a thousand-year-old relic of a mosque, forts, handicraft villages and ancient ports remain, reminding Bahrainis and visitors alike of the history, culture and heritage of this country—a history spanning many millennia.

A Brief History

Ancient times	Bahrain is inhabited between 50,000 and 100,000 years ago when it is still part of the mainland.
	A Sumerian text known as the epic of Gilgamesh refers to Dilmun (paradise), now identified as Bahrain. (Gilgamesh, a semi-mythical king, is supposed to have lived around 2600 BC.) The village of Saar, Barbar temple, the foundations of Bahrain fort and burial mounds date from this era.
8th century BC–6th century AD	In 710 BC, Sargon II of Assyria records that he received a tribute from King Uperi of Dilmun. Around 640 BC, the Persians conquer the island. It becomes part of the Babylonian empire 40 years later. In the 4th century BC, two of Alexander the Great's ships reach Bahrain, which the Greeks name Tylos. In the 1st century AD, Pliny records that Tylos is renowned for its abundance of pearls. In the 4th century the Sassanian king of Persia, Shappur II, annexes the island. Many inhabitants adopt Christianity.
7th–14th centuries	Around 630 the ruler is invited by the Prophet Mohammed to convert to Islam. He does so and many Bahrainis follow his example. In the 9th century, Bahrain, now a dependency of the Caliphate, becomes a centre of Carmathian rule (a radical Shiite sect). In 1058 a Bahraini resident, Abil-Bahloul, leads a revolt against the Carmathians and proclaims himself prince, but he is soon driven out by Yahya bin Abbas, the ruler of a neighbouring state, Qatif. The Moorish geographer Idrisi writes in 1154 that Bahrain "is governed by an independent chief. The inhabitants of the two banks are satisfied with his justice and his piety."

15

15th–17th centuries	Oman takes the island in 1487 but it is soon liberated by the Portuguese. They are are driven out at the beginning of the 17th century and the island comes under Persian rule.
18th–19th centuries	Ahmed al Fatih takes over Bahrain in 1783 and establishes the Al-Khalifa dynasty. His sons Salman and Abdulla sign a treaty with the British East Indian Company in 1820. In 1861 a Treaty of Perpetual Peace and Friendship is signed with Britain; the document assures Bahrain against external threats and underscores its position as a Protectorate of Britain.
	The accession of Shaikh Isa bin Ali as ruler in 1869 heralds a period of stability and prosperity.
20th century	In the 1930s, under Shaikh Hamad bin Isa, the first electric power station is built, a telephone system established, oil is discovered, the first aircraft lands. Shaikh Isa bin Salman Al-Khalifa succeeds his father on the throne in 1961. Ten years later Bahrain declares its independence; instead of joining the newly formed United Arab Emirates, Bahrain signs a new friendship treaty with Britain and joins the United Nations.

Sightseeing

Manama

Bahrain's capital of 150,000 is a combination of sleek, modern buildings encircled by broad avenues, and narrow lanes meandering through the bazaars.

The landmark, **Bab Al-Bahrain**, is the hub of the city. Designed in 1945 by Sir Charles Belgrave, Britain's political agent to the emirate, the Bab ("gate") initially served the customs operations. Today it houses the Directorate of Tourism, a shop of local handicrafts, an outdoor café and a tourist information office. It is also gateway to the **souk**, that fascinating labyrinth of streets and alleyways where shops and stalls sell anything from spices and tobacco leaves to stereos and cameras. It's a delightful place to amble, to absorb local colour, to take in the exotic scents and cacophony. Many visitors make a beeline for the Gold Souk on Shaikh Abdulla Avenue, an imposing three-floor granite edifice flanked by dozens of shops also selling gold, gems and precious metals in dazzling displays.

The **Heritage Centre**, a villa on Al-Khalifa Avenue, was built in the 1930s as the Law

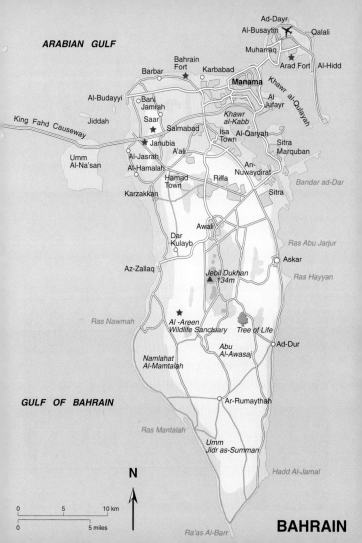

Courts. It is well worth a visit for its exhibits relating to pearl diving, fishing, falconry, modern art, music and weapons.

Ideal for strollers is the **Al-Awadiya** (wind-tower district) which boasts the Gulf's largest concentration of the traditional wind-cooling structures. At the beginning of the century, the first mansions began to spring up in this neighbourhood, most with expansive, palm-shaded courtyards. Sadly, many of the homes are now dilapidated, but characteristic architectural features are still evident.

Perhaps the best example of a wind-tower residence is the renovated **mansion** of the Ali Reza family with its grand portico and immense, leaning tower. Before modern air-conditioning arrived in Bahrain in the 1960s, the wind tower was an effective method of keeping the rooms cool.

Near the entrance to the Muharraq causeway, the **National Museum**, built in 1988, is a splendid place to learn more of the island's culture and history. Ancient archaeological artefacts are on display, including stea-

Beautifully carved doors make an imposing entrance to some of Bahrain's old houses.

tite seals and pots, and glass bottles recovered from burial mounds, as well as an entire burial mound thousands of years old. Dioramas depict local customs and Bahrain's recent pre-industrial past. One of the most striking additions to the museum is a hall of dinosaurs in a setting reminiscent of *Jurassic Park*.

Located in a former technical school, built in the 1930s, the **Bahrain Craft Centre** is managed by local women. In its fascinating workshops, you can watch the manufacture of paper from palm branches, as well as wool-weaving and stained-glass, among a dozen crafts.

Among the hundreds of mosques in Bahrain, the most imposing must be the **Al-Fateh Grand Mosque** on Al-Fateh Highway. With space for 7,000 worshippers, it is the island's largest building. Two free-standing minarets soar 70 m (230 ft) heavenwards while the great dome spans a diameter of 24 m (57 ft). Blending modern and traditional Islamic designs, the cavernous mosque is air-conditioned from underground ducts. Italian marble, an enormous Austrian chandelier and a giant wall-to-wall Scottish carpet complete the décor.

The restored **Al-Khamis mosque**, on Shaikh Salman Highway, attest to what is believed to be one of the oldest mosques in the Gulf. Possibly founded in the 7th century, the mosque possesses two striking minarets, which are said to date from the 15th century.

A replica of a Khamis minaret is found as part of the **Koran House** *(Beit Al-Quran),* at the eastern end of Government Avenue. This is the modern home of a priceless collection of Korans, ancient 7th to 8th-century parchments and writing instruments, illuminated tomes, computerized Koranic print-outs, verses on rice kernels and a huge, bound Koran from India, all in distinctive styles of Arabic calligraphy.

The **Andalus** and **Sulmaniya gardens**, one opposite the other on either side of Shaikh Isa Avenue, are pleasant parks to relax and contemplate Arabia. Late afternoon and evening, many families head for two popular amusement parks: the **Water Garden** and **Adhari**, built round a fresh-water spring. Both have fun-park rides and entertainment to enjoy with candyfloss and a bag of popcorn.

Golf is an increasingly popular sport in the Gulf. Bahrain's nine-hole **Golf Club** is a refreshingly green oasis as one heads into the desert.

19

Island Sights

Most villages in Bahrain specialize in a handicraft or two, passed down for countless generations. Baskets, floor mats and reed chicken coops, very much a part of the household, are produced in **Karbabad** where you'll notice one or two weavers at work at the side of the road. Close by is the **Bahrain Fort**. Though the Portuguese were the last important tenants of the bulwark (some locals refer to it as the Portuguese Fort), archaeologists have discovered no fewer than six foundations on the site, the earliest dated around 2800 BC. In ancient times, the fort's position on the western shores of Bahrain was a key vantage point for checking the advance of marauders.

If the site of Bahrain Fort was the ancient capital of Dilmun, **Barbar** is believed to be the sacred city, probably dating to 2200 BC. In the first of three temples, a holy well dedicated to Enki, god of fresh water, was built directly over a freshwater spring. A copper bull's head was certainly one of the most remarkable finds on the site. Steatite seals with fanciful designs of warriors, animals and marriage rites, hardly more than an inch (2.5 cm) in diameter, indicate that trading went on here at the time.

In the village of **Bani Jamrah**, textile weavers use hand looms to produce colourful fabrics that local ladies find irresistible. In an eight- to ten-hour working day, a weaver can fashion six metres of cloth.

Small camel herds may be viewed grazing on scrub in the dunes. The camel farm at **Janubia** is a delightful place to meet those four-footed friends of the desert.

Amid the sites and sights of Bahrain, the 25-km (15-mile) **King Fahd Causeway** linking the island with Saudi Arabia is a modern engineering marvel. When completed in 1986 at a cost of $1 billion, the causeway ended 8,000 years of separation from the mainland and heralded a boom in tourism from the kingdom and beyond. A panoramic view of the coastlines of the two countries is possible from a Disneyesque restaurant tower on the customs island at the causeway's midway point.

The causeway approach road runs past the village of **Saar**. Of all the country's archaeological sites, the dig at Saar is the most exciting, an ongoing excavation of an entire 2300 BC village, complete with temple, main street and two-room habitations. It's hoped that continuing research will unlock many of the mysteries still surrounding the period—why, for example, did the people vanish from the town around 1700 BC? Ancient Saar is located about 4 m (13 ft) beneath the present ground level.

Some 170,000 **burial mounds** scattered over the northern part of the island once marked the final resting place for nobles and commoners alike from as

A good way to keep cool in Bahrain's hot climate.

Traditional wooden boats carry tourists to dine beneath concrete turrets.

far back as the third millennium BC. Today the tumuli number only a few tens of thousands, victims over the centuries of vandalism and urbanization. There are around 15,000 in the neighbourhood of Saar but the largest mounds, including the Royal Tombs, are near **A'ali**, a village also renowned for its potters. Much of their craft finds its way into local homes, from bowls and vases to hookah pipes and a local version of a piggy bank.

Riffa has been the residence of the emir since 1956. You may catch a glimpse of the unostentatious palace of Bahrain's ruler from Shaikh Salman Highway.

The road continues south to **Awali**. This town was planned in 1934 for the foreign employees of the fledgling oil company. Today, it boasts a social club, tennis courts, a sand-dune golf course and many other creature comforts among neighbourhoods of villas with well-tended lawns. Away to the east, you can see the extensive plants of the Bahrain oil and gas industries.

A ribbon of road leads into the desert, the terrain becoming more desolate as villages slip from sight. **Jebil Dukhan** ("smoky mountain") looms over the expanse of dunes, at only 134 m (440 ft), Bahrain's highest point. Under the shadow of the *jebil* is the Gulf's first oil well, which struck black gold in 1932, an event that marked the advent of drastic changes in the economy as well as in the destiny of the country and, indeed, the entire region. The story of the industry's development over more than six decades is recounted through exhibits and photos in the nearby **oil museum**.

As you drive along the barren sandscape south of Dukhan, suddenly a great spreading tree appears on the horizon. The source of the **Tree of Life**'s water remains an enigma. Local lore says the gnarled mesquite is as old as the Garden of Eden, though hard-headed botanists place its age at around 400 years. Flints dating from the Stone Age were discovered in the vicinity.

A varied collection of wildlife is nurtured in the **Al-Areen wildlife reserve**, home to scores of the region's indigenous animals—and others. The Arabian

---

Gems from the deep

Clad in a thin cotton garment to protect him from jellyfish stings, a clip made of ram's horn on his nose, leather thimbles on his fingers and big toes, stone-weighted ropes tied to his feet and another rope round his waist, the pearl diver jumped into the sea and stayed under at a depth of 15 m (48 ft) for 60 seconds—until a tug at the rope warned him it was time to be hauled back up to the surface. In his bag, a dozen oysters. With luck, they would yield some of the highest quality natural pearls in the world—transformed, some believed, from raindrops caught by the mollusc during storms. After ten jumps, he could stay aboard and take a rest, warm up with a cup of coffee while another diver would take his place.

Year after year, from May to October, the pearl fishermen lived off shore over the pearl banks, their supplies ferried out by dhow. Divers and pullers would get their share of the profits, but only the merchants grew rich. Until oil was struck in 1932, pearling was the mainstay of the Bahraini economy. The industry collapsed in the 1940s, when the Japanese started to produce cultured pearls in earnest.

One thing is sure: if you buy pearls in Bahrain they will be the genuine article. Importation of the cultivated counterfeit is strictly forbidden.

oryx, virtually extinct in the wild, is a guest of honour in the reserve, but there are also zebras, iguanas, black swans, ostriches, flamingos and other exotic fauna.

Muharraq

The second largest of Bahrain's islands, Muharraq is dominated by the sprawling international airport, inaugurated in 1932 and linked to Manama by a causeway 7.5 km (4.5 miles) long. Once a bastion against invaders and a seat of government, Muharraq today still possesses many vestiges of its past. The patrician homes of Shaikh Isa and the Siyadi family (Ahmad Siyadi was an affluent pearl merchant) are a stone's throw from one another—both modest but noble dwellings.

The 26-room **Shaikh Isa house** (named for the emir who ruled from 1869 to 1923), built around 1800, is divided into four areas, each with its own courtyard and well: the emir's quarters, those for the women, for visitors and for the servants. Dating from 1900, **Ahmad Siyadi's home** is covered in artistic flourishes, both inside and out. The façade is adorned with heart-shaped crenellation, delicate symmetrical plasterwork, carved corners and an intricate portal piece. In the **dhow-building yards** where the traditional teak or mangrove sea-going vessels are constructed, still largely using non-electric tools. Having plied the seas of the region for centuries, the dhow transports both passengers and cargo as well as being used by fishermen and pearl divers.

Arad Fort (named after Arados, the Greek name for the island) was built in an Arabic style in the 16th century as part of a strategic network of bastions of defence against invaders. The Portuguese occupied Arad Fort from 1559 to 1635. The bulwark could hold enough provisions to maintain 300 soldiers for up to three months.

Eating Out

For centuries, Bahrain has had ties with the Indian sub-continent, so it's no wonder that Indian and Pakistani restaurants abound—whether vegetarian or so-called non-vegetarian. Rice —most often a delightfully aromatic basmati—predominates on menus with endless variety in rich sauces. You may go ethnic, eating with your hands, scooping up spicy morsels with freshly made naan or chapatti

Bahrain's children look cheerfully forward to the future.

Behave yourself!

Visitors to the Gulf countries should observe a few elementary rules of etiquette to avoid offending their Muslim hosts.

- In town, dress modestly: women should avoid clothes that may be considered revealing.
- Do not dress up in a *thobe*.
- Do not take photographs of people without their permission.
- If you have an appointment, be punctual.
- If you enter a room full of people, it is normal to shake hands with everyone. But men should not shake the hand of an Arab women unless she takes the initiative (and she may well not).
- If someone other than the coffee boy enters the room, stand up.
- It is polite to enquire about a man's family but not about his wife.
- Do not sit so that the soles of your shoes are pointing at someone.
- Only the right hand may be used for presenting gifts, touching and eating.
- Do not admire any of a man's possessions too enthusiastically; he may insist on giving it to you, and it would be offensive to refuse
- If you are offered coffee or tea, do not refuse. You should not drink more than three cups.
- Do not ask for alcoholic drinks.
- Refer to the Gulf as the Arabian, not the Persian, Gulf.

bread. To tame mouth-searing dishes, ask for yoghurt, not water.

The traditional Arabic dishes from the Levant are also readily available, from selections of *mezzeh* (as appetizers, they can turn into a full meal, for it isn't easy to know when to stop), shish-kebabs and sweet concoctions.

In addition to international cuisine, hotels usually have restaurants specializing in French, Italian, Japanese, Lebanese or Mexican dishes, among others. Live entertainment is often pro-vided, from high-decibel disco to gentle conventional dinner melodies.

Venturing out to some of the island's fine restaurants can be rewarding. Whether you prefer Thai or Tex-Mex, steaks or seafood, Bahraini or Spanish, homely dining in an old villa or a gastronomic experience in a palatial hall, you're sure to find something to suit your tastes. Even the well-known fast-food eateries have found their way to this desert isle, so you can catch up on hamburgers and fried chicken if such is your

26

bent. However, do not miss out on local produce: succulent giant Gulf prawns, and *hammour* (monkfish or burbot), best simply grilled. Buffet meals are immensely popular—an ideal way to sample many dishes at a time.

Even the most cosmopolitan coffee connoisseur is unlikely to have savoured the traditional Gulf brew. Here, coffee *(gahwah)* is prepared with the addition of cardamom and rose water. A generous pinch of saffron transforms the murky beverage into an aromatic tea-coloured drink. When you've had enough, wiggle the cup from side to side and return it to the server. Locally grown dates are usually served with *gahwah*.

Shopping

Many come to Bahrain to hunt for bargains in photographic and stereo equipment or household appliances. Others are looking for locally produced wares, or cassettes of Gulf music. The souvenir shop in the Bab Al-Bahrain is a good starting point for an array of mementoes, from T-shirts to hope chests.

If clumsy baggage is no problem, handmade dhow models and beautifully woven baskets make attractive gifts. Easier to pack into a suitcase are reed floor mats, fabrics and local apparel, from a robe *(thobe)* to a cape *(besht)*. Indian saris, colourful silk scarves and Omani incense are sought after by the locals. Perfume shops specialize in local essences which can be blended to suit your taste. Henna, believed to strengthen hair growth, is also used here for decorating women's hands and feet for special occasions. Home cooks will delight in the range of pungent spices which can be bought from the sack.

The Gold Souk is an ideal area to hunt for jewellery fashioned from precious metals, pearls and gems. Bahrain is noted for the high quality of the natural pearls produced here.

Attractive greeting cards with Islamic symmetrical designs and romantic scenes of old Arabia, mounted commemorative stamps and coins and books on Bahrain are also available at the post office or speciality shops.

Though set prices may exist for common wares, haggling is customary for most items. "How much is the discount?" may be the magic phrase to bring a price down slightly. Hard bargaining is needed for more expensive merchandise.

Those who love snooping around flea markets may find some knick-knack of value at Manama's Friday market.

Practical Information

Photos: Deyana Ahmadi

Clothing. Bahrain is Western in its approach to everyday life and, although some Bahraini women feel more comfortable in traditional *abbaya*, no formal dress code is imposed. Common sense should prevail. In towns and villages, shorts are frowned upon for both women and men. Women are advised to wear dresses or blouses to cover the shoulders and back, with a modest neckline. From November to March, you'll need a sweater or jacket in the evening. From June to October, you'll be glad you packed light-weight clothing and wash-and-wear fabrics.

Currency. The monetary unit is the *dinar* (BD), divided into 1000 *fils*. Notes are in denominations from 500 fils to 20 dinars; coins from 5 to 100 fils. Some vendors try to give Saudi *riyals* when making change; these are usually accepted like Bahraini currency. But BD1 equals 10 riyals. If this is more arithmetic than you care to handle, politely insist on Bahraini dinars.

Hours. The weekend begins Thursday afternoon and ends Friday evening. Government offices are open 7 a.m.–2.15 p.m. Saturday to Wednesday. Banks, however, open 7.30 a.m. until noon Saturday to Wednesday, until 11 a.m. Thursday. Shops, businesses and currency-exchange offices generally open 8 a.m. until 1 p.m., then close for a siesta until 3 or so. Shops usually close at 6 or 7 p.m. But on Wednesdays and Thursdays, late-night shopping keeps stores open until at least 9 p.m. Friday mornings, some shops do business.

Language. While the official language is Arabic, English is widely understood.

Photography. Be sensitive about taking pictures of local people, who may be offended.

Religion. Islam is practised by 85% of the population. As a tolerant society, the country has several other faiths represented. During the month of Ramadan, out of respect to fasting Muslims, tourists must not eat, drink or smoke in public during daylight hours. But shops and restaurants stay open into the early hours of the morning. Every international hotel, however, will have a restaurant open during the daytime for non-Muslims.

QATAR

Arabian Sands

If you thought sand was just something gritty that gets into the sandwiches, you'll soon learn otherwise in Qatar. From tip to base, much of this thumb of land jutting into the emerald waters of the Arabian Gulf is desert, varying from grey dust blowing around the towns and villages, through heavy golden packed deposits easily navigated by camels, to rippling red drifts, draped and smoothed by the winds into high dunes.

Between Saudi Arabia and the United Arab Emirates, the State of Qatar is a little smaller than Northern Ireland. For hundreds of years the Qataris lived quietly from fishing and pearling, governed by the strict Islamic law, or Shari'a, based on the Quran. The capital, Doha, was hardly more than a dusty village of 12,000 inhabitants, living for the most part in tumble-down stone dwellings. Shops and bazaars huddled together in a maze of covered lanes.

Oil was discovered in 1939, and today more than four-fifths of the national income comes from oil and gas production. In just half a century the country has taken a tremendous leap into the industrial age. Doha has burgeoned into a glittering town of square-cut, concrete banks and agencies, hotels, embassies and ministries set along straight, broad avenues. It spreads round a wide, semicircular bay on the east coast, just above the joint of the thumb. The car is king here, and most of the efforts to beautify the city amount to monumental roundabouts adorned with symbolic studies of coffee pots, rose-water sprinklers and so on, landscaped with fountains and greenery.

Though the men still wear their white robes with pride and most of the women dress modestly in black, they are hardly backward-looking; girls far outnumber boys in secondary schools and university education. The population is nearly half a million, but only a quarter are Qatari, the rest being Pakistanis, Lebanese, Sudanese, Palestinians, Egyptians, Syrian, Jordanians and Europeans. A great majority live in Doha, the others in a few coastal villages or the one oil refinery town of Umm Said, thankfully tucked out of sight down the coast.

The climate is hot, and in summer most people stay inside in air-conditioned comfort. But from September to June, basking in wintry warmth and soaking up spring sunshine can be exhilarating in a land where a rainy day is as rare as an oasis.

A Brief History

Early times	The peninsula is inhabited during the Stone Age. In the 5th century BC, Greek historian Herodotus describes the inhabitants as being originally sea-faring Canaanites.
2nd century AD	Geographer Ptolemy places Catara (or Catra) on his map, probably locating the present-day town of Zubarah.
7th century	The Qatar peninsula and surrounding region are ruled by the Al-Mundhir Arabs. Their king Al-Mundhir Ibn Sawi Al-Tamimi converts to Islam.
8th century	Qatar is ruled by the Abbasids under the Caliph of Baghdad, resulting in great prosperity.
16th–17th centuries	Power struggles are played out in the Gulf between Portuguese, British, Dutch and French who scrap over the monopoly of trade routes to India and the Far East. The initial settlers remain on the coast living from fishing, trading and pearl diving. The nomadic Bedouins roam the interior. In 1617 Qatar comes first under Portuguese control which lasts for 21 years, then under the Turks.
18th–19th centuries	A tribal group including the Al-Thani family arrives in the north of Qatar during the early 18th century. They move to Doha in the middle of the 19th century under the leadership of Mohammed bin Thani. In 1867 Commander Lewis Pelly, British political resident in the Gulf, recognizes Sheikh Mohammed as the peninsula's most influential man and signs a peace agreement with him. The document gives the sheikh responsibility for the security of the seas. In 1871 Sheikh Mohammed agrees with Midhat Pasha, the Turkish ruler of Iraq, to admit an Ottoman military force into the country, and Qatar becomes a Turkish administrative district. Sheikh Qassim, Sheikh Mohammed's son, leads the way to unity of the country.
20th century	The Turks leave in 1913. Sheikh Qassim's successor Abdullah sides with Britain in World War I. In 1916 Britain and Qatar sign a protection treaty. Oil is discovered in 1939, and the first oil exported in 1949. Independence is declared on 3 September 1971, ending British sovereignty over Qatar. Sheikh Khalifa bin Hamad Al-Thani, officially enthroned as amir in 1972, is deposed by his son Hamad bin Khalifa in 1995.

Sightseeing

Doha

Doha's palm-lined **Corniche**, a sea-front promenade, sweeps grandly for 4 miles (7 km) round its bay. All the important sights are enclosed between this road and A Ring Road, the first of three concentric highways embracing the city.

East along the Corniche, near the intersection with Al-Muthaf Street, most of what remains of Qatar's history is gathered together in the **National Museum**. Housed in the former palace of Sheikh Abdulla Bin Mohammed who ruled from 1913 to 1951, the displays are arranged without any apparent logical order, in a labyrinth of rooms, corridors and courtyards. They fascinate Qataris as much as outside visitors, reviving forgotten memories of life before oil. Particularly interesting is a Bedouin tent complete with carpets, embroidered cushions and coffee pot, looking for all the world as though the family is about to return at any minute. There's a gallery devoted to the oil industry, and outside, beautifully restored wooden dhows floating on a lagoon. Live local fish such as sharks and stingrays can be viewed from a reasonable distance. The museum is closed on Friday morning and all day Saturday; Tuesday afternoons are reserved for families.

A walk along Jasim Bin Mohammed Street, from the Corniche towards the town centre, will take you past the landmark Clock Tower and the many-domed Grand Mosque to **Doha Fort**. Admission is free to this old building where you can buy traditional Bedouin handicrafts. In neighbouring Al-Najada Street, next to a parking lot, one of the few remaining Qatari houses with a **windtower** has been restored. You can sit beneath the tower and feel the cooling effect of this ingenious ecological invention.

Opposite is the entrance to the **souk**. Venture into its alleyways for some fascinating insight into the Arabian way of life, even if you're not looking for a goat or tobacco leaves.

North Coast

On the coast, 41 miles (67 km) north of Doha, **Al Khor** is a small pleasant town built around a dhow harbour. The **museum**, formerly a port police station, boasts archaeological artefacts from the vicinity going back several millennia. Several old **watchtowers** on the harbour have been restored. Established in 1963, the **Rawdat al Faras** experimental farm is an attempt to turn the desert green by culti-

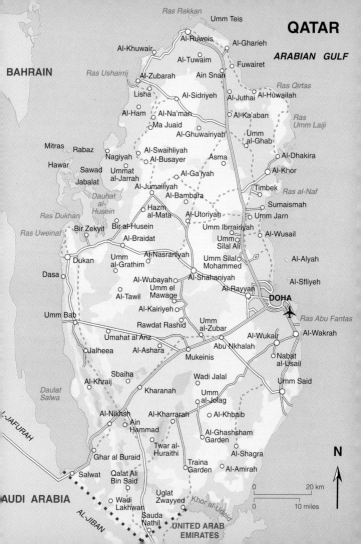

QATAR

ARABIAN GULF

BAHRAIN

Ras Rakkan
Umm Teis
Al-Ruweis
Al-Gharieh
Al-Khuwair
Al-Tuwaim
Fuwairet
Ras Ushairrij
Al-Zubarah
Ain Snan
Ras Qirtas
Lisha
Al-Sidriyeh
Al-Juthai
Al-Huwailah
Al-Ham
Al-Na'man
Al-Ka'aban
Ras Umm Laiji
Ma Juaid
Al-Ghuwairiyah
Umm al-Ghab
Mitras
Rabaz
Nagiyah
Al-Swaihliyah
Al-Busayer
Asma
Al-Dhakira
Hawar
Sawad
Ummat al-Jarrah
Al-Ga'lyah
Al-Khor
Jabalat
Al-Jumailiyah
Timbek
Ras al-Naf
Dauhat al-Husein
Al-Bambara
Sumaismah
Ras Dukhan
Hazm al-Mata
Al-Utoriyah
Umm Jarn
Ras Uweinat
Bir al-Husein
Umm Ibrrairiyah
Al-Wusail
Bir Zekyit
Al-Braidat
Umm Silal Ali
Dukan
Al-Nasraniyah
Umm Silal Mohammed
Al-Alyah
Umm al-Grathim
Dasa
Al-Wubayah
Al-Shahaniyah
Al-Sfliyeh
Umm el Mawage
Al-Rayyan
Al-Tawil
DOHA
Umm Bab
Al-Kairiyeh
Ras Abu Fantas
Rawdat Rashid
Umm al-Zubar
Umahat al Anz
Al-Wukair
Al-Wakrah
Jalheea
Al-Ashara
Abu Nkhalah
Nabat al-Usail
Mukeinis
Sbaiha
Wadi Jalal
Umm Said
Al-Khraij
Kharanah
Umm al-Jolag
Daulat Salwa
Al-Nikhsh
Al-Kharrarah
Al-Khbaib
AL-JAFURAH
Ain Hammad
Al-Ghashsham Garden
Twar al-Huraithi
Al-Shagra
Ghar al Buraid
Traina Garden
Al-Amirah
Salwat
Qalat Ali Bin Said
AUDI ARABIA
Wadi Lakhwan
Uglat Zwayyed
Khor al-Udeid
AL-JIBAN
Sauda Nathil
UNITED ARAB EMIRATES

N

0   20 km

0   10 miles

vating fruits and vegetables in a hot, dry climate. There's a picnic area with restaurants and barbecue facilities at **Al Khor Gardens**, just past the turnoff for Al Khor from the North Road.

Al Ruweis, at the northern tip of the peninsula, was once the port of call for a ferry service from Bahrain. Its clear waters are host to several varieties of coral and tropical fish. One of the homes here is often open to visitors, to sit in the carpeted *majlis* (living room), sip sweetened tea or coffee, and meet the family falcons on their outside perch. Women visitors are permitted to enter the ladies' part of the house where they can make acquaintance with Qatari women.

The beaches in the Al Ruweis region are very popular for all kinds of aquatic activities, from snorkelling to jet-skiing.

Zubarah was Qatar's most important settlement until a century ago. Now it's virtually abandoned, visited occasionally by Qataris on falconing expeditions. The **fort**, built in 1938 as a coast-guard lookout, was transformed into a museum in 1987. A rectangular edifice with three round towers and one square, crenellated bastion, it affords sweeping views of the landscape—over the empty desert and out over the sea, as far as Bahrain on a clear day. Several of the rooms around the courtyard display archaeological artefacts dating as far back as 5000 BC. Nearby excavations reveal walls of dwellings from the Abassidian era of the 8th century AD.

The South

The pearl-diving centre of **Wakrah** is only a 20-minute drive from Doha. One of its traditional houses near the harbour has been restored and now serves as a **museum** on marine life (Tuesday afternoons are reserved for families). There are some ruins behind it, thought to be a palace.

Beyond the city of Umm Said, hub of the steel and petrochemical industries, the **desert** sprawls endlessly in all directions. Only the occasional apparition of camels on the horizon relieves the infinite landscape of sand and dunes, more sand and more dunes, billowing in great waves and swells. Dune-driving and sand-skiing have become popular sports in recent times, the skiers lifted to the top of the 130-ft (40 m) dunes by four-wheel drive.

After a bumpy ride southwards, with only a compass to indicate the way, you suddenly encounter the so-called inland

34

sea of **Khor-Al-Udeid** appearing like a mirage. This body of water is not a freshwater lake but a saltwater inlet linked to the Gulf by a channel 4 miles (7 km) long. Virtually on the Saudi Arabia border, Khor-Al-Udeid is a paradise for hanggliders, snorkellers, snorkellers, swimmers, anglers and even for lazy sunbathers.

After a hard day of sun and fun at Khor-Al-Udeid, you can return to Doha by the coast road, less arduous than the more direct dunes route.

Eating Out

Doha has a wide selection of restaurants specializing in Arabian, Asian and European food —and American fast-food outlets have found their way here, too. With so many Asians living in Qatar, it's no wonder that the cooking of that continent dominates, from spicy Indian dishes to wok-sautéed Far Eastern delights. But if you prefer to dine *à la française* or stick to more familiar European dishes, you'll have no problem finding the right place to eat. To venture beyond the comfortable surroundings of a hotel into a good local restaurant can be a rewarding experience.

Qataris love buffet meals, which are a wonderful way to pick and choose both well-known and exotic dishes. You could make a whole meal from *mezze* (starters) alone. The array of hot and cold appetizers is irresistible, from *tabbouleh* (cracked wheat, tomato and parsley salad), *kibbeh* (pine-nut filled meatball) and *samosa* (vegetable or meat-filled pasties) to *muktabal* (aubergine dip), *hommous* (chick pea dip) and *dolmas* (stuffed vine leaves).

But save room for the kebabs of chicken, meat or fish; the tasty rice-casserole main dishes and the tender, succulent whole baked lamb *(oozi)*.

Qataris have a sweet tooth, and *uma'ali* (bread pudding) and dates and bananas in cream are among favourites.

Shopping

Most souk merchandise can be haggled over, whether it's spices or stereos, gold or goats. Hand-worked jewellery is a particularly good buy, attractively priced in the gold souk.

If you're comparing prices on home appliances, textiles, perfumes, electronic goods and TV and video equipment, visit Doha's shopping centres which stock products from Europe, the United States and the Far East. Al Saad Street is the best place to start.

If you want to take home something typical of Arabia, you might consider the characteristic Gulf coffee pots with pointed spouts, the unusual rose-water sprinklers, or slip-on sandals. Carpets, silk scarves and exotic, locally blended essences for perfumes are also sought after.

Photo: Qatar National Hotels Co.

Practical Information

Clothing. Light, loose-fitting cotton garments are best in Qatar's hot climate. You can dress up for meals in some of Qatar's elegant dining rooms. In public, however, bear in mind that you're in an Islamic country where customs should be respected. Miniskirts for women and shorts for men are out of place in the streets. On the beach or at the pool, usual bathing attire is acceptable, but women cannot go topless.

Currency. The *riyal*, expressed as QR, is divided into 100 *dirhams*. Notes from 1 to 500 riyals; coins 25 and 50 dirhams. Currency exchanges in town generally give a more favourable rate than hotels.

Hours. The weekend begins on Thursday afternoon and lasts all day Friday. Government offices are open Saturday to Thursday from 7 a.m. to 1 p.m., while banks open at 8 a.m. and close at noon. Most shops and businesses operate on a two-shift system, from 8 a.m. to 12.30 p.m. and from 4 to 8.30 p.m.

Language. While the official language is Arabic, English is widely understood.

Photography. Always ask permission before taking pictures of the local inhabitants, who may take offence.

Religion. The Qataris belong to the Wahabi sect of Islam and practise strict fundamentalism. During the month of Ramadan, out of respect to fasting Muslims, tourist must not eat, drink or smoke in public during daylight hours—though at night business is as usual. However, every international hotel will have a restaurant open during the day for non-Muslims.

UNITED
ARAB EMIRATES

Arabian Days

An ancient people in a young country is how the United Arab Emirates (UAE) sees itself. On the surface, it is the new that dominates. The ultra-modern cities are filled with luxurious hotels and amazingly high-tech skyscrapers of coloured glass and concrete, everything in mint condition. The country is criss-crossed by six-lane highways along which vast limousines and land-cruisers speed with nonchalant ease. The shops are crammed to the ceiling with the most up-to-date computers and cameras. This is the fabulous world of the Thousand-and-One Nights, transformed into an Arabian California.

But the visitor should beware of making hasty judgements. Look inside the limousine and you will see the driver is wearing a *dishdasha* (the traditional white robe). He might just as likely be going to a falcon hunt at a remote oasis as a business meeting at the office. And just beyond the modern skyline is the haunting grandeur of the timeless desert. The camel may have been displaced as the major mode of transport, but this is still a desert society, profoundly connected to the most famous product of that desert culture, the Koran and Islam.

Indeed, it is remarkable to think that the astounding economic transformation which confronts the visitor has been brought about by an essentially conservative Muslim society. For all that, the result of this blend of the ancient and the new is a genuinely cosmopolitan environment where, true to the ways of the Bedouin, the traveller is always welcome.

Of course, things have been smoothed along by the discovery of oil. Before it came on stream in 1962, the Gulf was struggling as one of the poorest places on earth, with Abu Dhabi the poorest of all the sheikh-doms of the Trucial Coast (it is now the wealthiest). The coastal population lived from fishing and pearl diving (though Dubai had long been a busy trading centre). In the interior, the Bedouins scratched a meagre living from subsistence farming and camel-herding, as well as less salubrious pursuits such as raiding and extorting money from passing caravans. Nor were matters helped by the long-standing hostilities among the various tribes in the region. Until relatively recently there have been raids and skirmishes even between the emirates themselves. The anticipation of finding more oil, together with the extremely eccentric borders that the British mapped out for the seven emirates, only added to the tension.

All the more remarkable then, that these days the UAE counts as one of the most politically stable countries in the Middle East, as well as being a refreshingly safe place to travel in. It has existed as a self-governing state only since 1971. Following the British decision to withdraw from the Gulf, the seven emirates recognized the uncomfortable fact of being very small and very wealthy minnows in a Gulf full of sharks, and consequently joined together to form one federated country. However, each emirate is fiercely independent, and each resists moves towards increased federal power with gusto.

The UAE comprises Abu Dhabi (capital and largest of the seven, with 85 per cent of the overall territory, and the only real oil state), Dubai, Sharjah (the main port of entry for tourists), Ajman, Umm al-Qaiwain, Ras al-Khaimah and Fujairah (the only emirate without a coastline on the Gulf). Within its total area of 83,600 sq km (32,300 sq miles) there is a population of 2.3 million, of whom 75 per cent are expatriate workers, mainly from the Indian sub-continent, South-East Asia and Europe.

The UAE's story has not been one of unhindered progress. The collapse of oil prices in the mid to late 1980s affected the smaller emirates severely as the richer ones were forced to cut back on their subsidies. The lesson learnt was that a country cannot rely on a single product forever, even one as profitable as oil.

A happy consequence of this has been the active welcoming of tourists and business travellers. The UAE has worked hard to make itself one of the most accessible places in the region for the foreign visitor. It has all the attractions and amenities a person might want from a major holiday destination—excellent hotels, historic sights and spectacular scenery, deep-sea fishing, scuba-diving and first-rate beaches, even championship-level golf courses. Not forgetting other particularly Arabian pleasures: don't miss the chance of a desert safari, or a helicopter ride across the sands. Better still, have a go at sand-skiing down a dune, or the popular wadi-bashing—speeding through dry riverbeds in 4-wheel-drive vehicles. On top of all this, for the dedicated shopper there are boundless opportunities—both in the up-to-date shopping malls and the traditional souk markets.

39

A Brief History

Prehistory	The Arabian Gulf coast comes under the influence of the civilizations of Mesopotamia and the Indus River. With East-West trade routes passing along the Gulf, goods from India and China reach the coastal communities and travel on to the interior by camel caravan.
16th–17th centuries	The Portuguese become the dominant power in the Gulf and remain so for over a century, taxing the Gulf's lucrative trade with India and the Far East. They seize the Kingdom of Hormuz (comprising much of what is today the UAE) and control the straits between the Arabian Gulf and the Gulf of Oman. In 1622 the British East India Company, with the Dutch and Persians, attack and eject the Portuguese from Hormuz. Around the mid-17th century the coastal communities of the lower Gulf are acquired by the imams of Oman.
18th century	The lower Gulf falls under Persian rule from 1720 to 1740. Decline of the Persian and Omani dynasties leads to a political vacuum which the British seek to fill.
19th century	Britain faces strong naval resistance from the al-Qawasim of Ras al-Khaimah. The lower Gulf is dubbed the Pirate Coast. After several British military actions, a final invasion in 1820 leads to peace treaties concluding with 1853 Treaty of Maritime Peace in Perpetuity. The lower Gulf coast is called the Trucial Coast. In 1892 "exclusive agreements" are signed between Britain and sheikhdoms guaranteeing protection in exchange for keeping rival European powers and Russia out of the Gulf. The Gulf's role as staging post for the route to India is enhanced.
20th century	The British leave India in 1947, weakening their need for a military presence east of Suez. In the 1960s vast oil revenues begin to flow in. In 1968 the British announce their intention to leave the region and the UAE is formed in December 1971. Dangers such as the fundamentalist regime in Iran and the Iran-Iraq war prompt the UAE, together with Oman, Qatar, Saudi Arabia, Bahrain and Kuwait, to form the Gulf Cooperation Council in 1981 to strengthen the security of the region and promote economic cooperation. In the 1991 Gulf War the UAE stands firm with the UN coalition against Iraq's invasion of Kuwait.

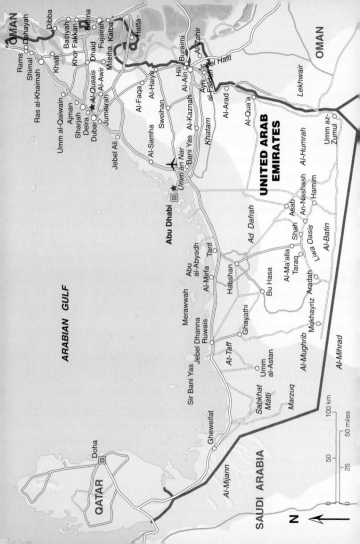

Sightseeing

Abu Dhabi

Crossing **Muqta Bridge**, you might be forgiven for thinking that the modern high-rise city ahead is a mirage, an illusory Arabian metropolis looming from the heat haze of the desert. Take a glance at its recent history and you may feel convinced you were right. The transformation that has taken place can only be described as magical. When the British explorer Wilfred Thesiger arrived here in 1948, he could reach the level, sandy island on which Abu Dhabi stands only at low tide and on camelback. What confronted him is hard to imagine now. "A large castle dominated the small dilapidated town which stretched along the shore. There were a few palms, and near them was a well where we watered our camels. Then we went over to the castle and sat outside the walls, waiting for the Sheikhs to wake from their afternoon slumbers." Even in the mid-1960s, the scene was not much different.

Today, however, the sheikhs have moved out to more luxurious, high-tech residences and the castle is dwarfed by the town and its brand-new skyscrapers. Perhaps the very fact of its survival makes it the most remarkable of all Abu Dhabi's architectural feats. The white-washed **Al-Husn Palace**, or White Fort, is in fact the oldest structure in the city, dating from the reign of the present ruler's grandfather, Zayed the Great (reigned 1855–1909). It replaced an earlier fort built just after the Al-Bu Falah tribe, who form the majority of Abu Dhabi's Arab population, first settled on the island at the end of the 18th century. What brought them here was the region's most precious commodity—not oil, but water. Legend has it that a group of hunters from the Liwa Oasis were led to a freshwater well by a deer they were chasing (Abu Dhabi means "father of the gazelle"). Although the truth is probably far less romantic, the ruling al-Nahyan dynasty made sure their fort was constructed over the well, as unambiguous an assertion of power as you could want. The fort now houses a document centre belonging to the Cultural Foundation. You are, however, free to walk around the courtyard and take advantage of your only chance to soak up the atmosphere of a bygone age in Abu Dhabi.

The spanking new face of Abu Dhabi.

Filled with datepalm trees, fountains and brilliant flowers, it is a true oasis in the noisy, bustling city.

The **Cultural Foundation** itself is a five-minute walk from the White Fort. Although its main function is as a library and research centre, it also holds lectures and exhibitions which are open to the public. Photography seems to be particularly popular, but the exhibitions may include paintings, local history displays, manuscripts, and so on. There is also a concert hall where performances range from Italian opera and Sri Lankan dancing to Arabic drama. You can obtain information about the month's events from the Cultural Foundation reception desk, which is open every day except Friday.

Just across Zayed the First Street is the **Grand Mosque**, an eye-catching mixture of Islamic architecture and Italianate white marble colonnades. You can walk through the gardens, but non-Muslims are not allowed to enter the mosque itself.

The best place to take in Abu Dhabi's modernistic façade is along the **Corniche**, a scenic promenade which stretches along the lagoon. Better still, look down on the waterfront from the 29th floor of the Baynunah Tower Hotel, the tallest building in Abu Dhabi, as you sip a freshly squeezed orange juice. Across the lagoon on a thin arm of land is **Breakwater Park**, a favourite place for watching the sunset and enjoying the breeze.

The Corniche is lined with the banks, 5-star hotels and oil company offices which represent the emirate's phenomenal economic growth since the 1970s. Abu Dhabi is now the financial centre and capital of the UAE. The reason for such success can be mulled over at the **Petroleum Exhibition**, on the east side of the city. Oil was first discovered in the Middle East—in Iran and Iraq—before World War I. After 1918, the Great Powers swooped on Arabia like hawks and snapped up prospecting concessions throughout the region. The impoverished sheikhs were only too happy for the cash: in 1933, Ibn Saud of Saudi Arabia haggled for £50,000 from Standard Oil against future royalties. The Abu Dhabi economy at this time was based on fishing and pearl-diving. Following the collapse of the wild pearl market in the 1930s, Sheikh Shakhbut (reigning 1928–1966) granted a concession to the British-owned Iraq Petroleum Company, and later, after the war, to an Anglo-French consortium. It was the

44

latter who discovered oil offshore in 1958. With a population of only 15,000 at the time, it was apparent that the nation was destined for great wealth. Sheikh Zayed bin Sultan al-Nahyan, the present ruler, assured this outcome by forming the Abu Dhabi National Oil Company (ADNOC) and nationalizing the earlier concessions. Abu Dhabi's oil reserves are good for at least another hundred years at current extraction rates, and its natural gas reserves are vast, so the party should last for some time yet. Through posters, documents, photographs, models and film shows, the exhibition will tell you all you want to know about how the flow of black gold changed Thesiger's sleepy watering hole forever.

Although the souks in Dubai are probably better for variety and atmosphere, you might want to check out the **Old Souk** just off the Corniche between Hamdan Street and Khalifa Street, where you can buy the latest electrical goods and also enjoy the aroma of spices and fruits. A huge new Grand Souk in the Medina Zayed area is destined to replace the older markets. You can investigate some bargain basement goods brought over from Iran by dhow (the traditional Arabian sailing boat), and sold at stalls beside the boats at the **Iranian Souk**, in Abu Dhabi's Free Port.

Just to the south of the city, on the road leading to the airport, the **Women's Craft Centre** exhibits and sells traditional woven fabrics, as well as other products of centuries-old crafts.

The settlement of Abu Dhabi may be relatively recent but some 4,000 years ago the area was the centre of a flourishing trading culture. In 1959 a team of Danish archaeologists discovered the remains of a Bronze Age port on the nearby island of **Umm an Nar**. Copper mined in the Hajar mountains was exported through here to the ancient Sumerian and other Mesopotamian civilizations. The Umm an-Nar culture extended deep into the interior of the country and lasted for centuries. In our present oil culture, however, the island is dominated by a large refinery.

In the "garden city" of **Al-Ain**, situated on the Buraimi oasis 160 km (100 miles) to the southeast, you will find more scenic and accessible archaeological sites possibly connected with the Umm an-Nar culture. The most spectacular is in the **Hili Gardens**, a popular municipal park. Surrounded by picnicking families and strolling couples is the remarkable 45

On the Round Tomb in the Hili Gardens, a couple linked together since the 3rd millenium BC.

Round Tomb dating from the 3rd millennium BC and only discovered in the late 1960s. Look for the poignant carving of two people holding hands beneath a couple of giant oryxes. The antelopes, with their fabulous curved horns, are one of the symbols of Arabia, but by the early 1970s they were virtually extinct. One positive aspect of Abu Dhabi's new-found wealth was the funding of an intensive effort to save the species. At the Al-Ain **zoo** you can witness the result: the largest collection of Arabian oryxes in the world.

Some have even been reintroduced into the wild. The zoo also contains a varied collection of other animals, including houbaras (Arabian bustards), lions, gazelles and hippos.

Al-Ain's **museum** pulls together under one roof the complex historical—and pre-historical—elements of the emirate. It contains many of the smaller artefacts found at Umm an-Nar, Hili, Jebel Hafit and other archaeological sites, such as Bronze Age weapons, jewellery and pottery. The informative explanatory labels and wall posters are in English as well as Arabic. There's an ethnographical display which concentrates on the country's proud Bedouin tradition (although the waxwork tribesmen are only involved in peaceful activities such as farming rather than their more famous martial exploits). In the first gallery, take time to study the excellent collection of photographs of the emirate in the 1960s. They are a fascinating record of the region's dramatic transformation.

The 18th-century **Eastern Fort**, immediately in front of the museum, was the birthplace of Sheikh Zayed, ruler of Abu Dhabi and President of the UAE. The fort looks splendidly exotic from the outside, although the walls enclose little more than an old cannon and the occasional grazing goat. The large new building in the style of a fort a few hundred yards from the museum is the **livestock souk**. This attracts buyers from all over southern UAE and northern Oman. To catch the best of the trading action make sure you're there early.

North of the city centre, the restored fortifications of the **Muraijib Fort** are located in an attractive landscaped park. The **Buraimi oasis** is dotted with forts of varying age—such as Muraijib, Muwaiji, Al-Khandaq

and Al-Hilla—reflecting its historic significance as a vital watering hole at an important desert crossroads. By the 10th century it was a major centre for trade on Arabia's caravan routes. In the 18th century it was briefly absorbed into the fledgling first Saudi Arabian empire, but this state soon disintegrated. A military invasion by the Saudis in the 1950s was repelled by Sheikh Zayed, then governor of Al-Ain, who led a Bedouin force in conjunction with the Trucial Oman Scouts under British officers.

The Al-Nahyans have ruled Al-Ain since the beginning of the century, during which time control of the whole oasis has been shared jointly with Oman. The border with Oman was finally demarcated in 1966, and you will be able to cross from one side to the other without a passport. The Omani town is called Buraimi. If you feel like travelling in a different country for an hour or two, the renovated **Al-Khandaq fort** is worth seeking out. It's at least 250 years old and very photogenic. Climb up to one of the turrets and you will be treated to an excellent view of the Omani part of the oasis. Further along the main road is the **Buraimi souk**, an atmospheric market selling mainly food, with a par- 47 ticularly enticing selection of fruit. Behind the souk is the run-down Al-Hilla fort, which is closed to the public.

Without doubt, though, the best souk on either side of the border is the one where you are least likely to buy anything. Back in Al-Ain the colourful **camel market**, open from early morning till around midday, is not to be missed. It is a glimpse of the old, Bedouin Arabia where, before the advent of the 4-wheel-drive, the camel held sway. The Bedouin called them *Ata Allah*, or "God's gift". They provided transport, milk, food, and their hair and hide became the raw material for household goods—even their shoulder blades were used as slates for schoolchildren to write on. The camel still has a part to play in the modern world, as the hard bargaining at the market demonstrates. The building nearby that looks like yet another fort is the **Old Prison**. If you can get up to the roof of the tower in-side (which unfortunately is often locked), you will be re-warded with a grandstand view of the camel market below.

For light relief, there's always **Hili Fun City**. Called, rather hopefully, the Disneyland of the Middle East, the Gulf's largest theme park can offer a looping rollercoaster, a Dynamic Mo-tion Theatre and an ice skating rink among its many attractions. The park is closed all day Satur-day.

Located to the south of Al-Ain, **Jebel Hafit** (Mount Hafit) is the highest point in the UAE. The road to the summit winds upwards for 9 km (5 miles), and when you finally reach the top you are truly in the heavens. The views from here are particu-larly breathtaking because Jebel Hafit is in fact an enor-mous rock from the Hajar mountain range set adrift in a vast desert plain. There is a spectacular bird's-eye view of Al-Ain. Immediately below are the wadis, the dry riverbeds, whose trails can be seen running down from the mountain and tapering off into the sands. And, looking west across to the Rub al-Khali, the Empty Quarter, there's nothing but the desert between you and Mecca more than a thousand miles away.

For a closer brush with the Empty Quarter head out to the **Liwa Oasis**, which stands on its very edge. This was the home of the emirate's dominant Al-Bu Falah tribe before they moved to Abu Dhabi. The oasis is near Abu Dhabi's Western Desert area, which contains most of its oilfields. For obvious reasons the authorities are very tight on security here—be careful where

48

you point your camera. Liwa is really a chain of some 30 small oases spread out along an arc dotted with separate villages. It is the centre of a huge project aimed at greening the desert; some of the plantations cover 200 sq km (77 sq miles). The high sand dunes around Liwa are famous for their dramatic beauty and once seen are not soon forgotten. Contemplating the vast, hypnotic sweep of the desert here, it is possible to understand Lawrence of Arabia's view that "this cruel land can cast a spell no temperate clime can match".

Dubai

As long ago as 1580, an Italian traveller reported that Dubai was a prosperous pearl-diving and fishing community. It was still much the same at the beginning of the 20th century, when over 300 pearl-diving dhows were stationed in Dubai's Creek. Modern Dubai can be said to date from the 1830s when 800 men of the Bani Yas tribe under the Al-Maktoum family settled here. The Al-Maktoums have ruled ever since and what's more seem to have been blessed in each generation with a leader of acute business acumen.

In 1894 the family began giving tax exemptions to foreign traders and in 1903 persuaded a British steamship company to use Dubai as the main port of call en route to India. When Sheikh Rashid took over, things really began to hot up. In the 1950s he invested heavily in dredging the Creek, which was beginning to silt up. The modernization programme continued with the decision to build Jebel Ali, the world's largest man-made port, and to develop Dubai's international airport, with its famously lavish duty-free area. Dubai's unbridled *laissez-faire* economy was encouraged, but crucially underpinned by considerable spending on infrastructure. It seems to have paid off. Dubai is not dependent on oil production for its success—less than a quarter of the emirate's wealth comes from petroleum exports. Instead, Sheikh Rashid emphatically achieved his ambition of making Dubai the region's leading trade centre: Dubai today accounts for 70 per cent of the UAE's imports and re-exports. He died in 1990 and was succeeded by his son, Sheikh Maktoum, who would seem to be keeping a steady hand on the tiller.

Dubai is really a tale of two cities. Bur Dubai and Deira are divided by the **Creek**, which runs inland from the Gulf for 49

about 10 km (6 miles) and once went as far as Al-Ain. It is the city's main artery, and its elegant serpentine curves and miraculously clear water provide the picturesque backdrop to one of the great sights of the UAE, the old teak trading dhows double-parked along the Deira side. Now powered by motor rather than sail, they bring goods to and from other parts of the Middle East and travel as far as India and East Africa. The waterfront hums with the excitement of trade and is crammed with their incredibly diverse cargoes. Here you will see American refrigerators and Japanese electronics unloaded alongside stacks of plastic garden chairs, sacks of rice and even the occasional spiral staircase bound for who-knows-where. Contributing to the general cacophony are the **abras**, or water taxis, which crisscross the Creek till late at night. Their captains call out to passers-by until the boat is full and can depart. This never takes long, and the abra is by far the most enjoyable and easiest way to make the crossing. If you want a tour of the Creek, there is no difficulty in hiring the whole

Crossing the Creek in the centre of Dubai.

abra by the hour. Special dhow tours can be arranged through hotels and tourist companies.

Dubai's reputation for trade can be tested almost as soon as you leave the Creek. Everywhere you look there are bargains to be had, but don't be shy—haggling is virtually obligatory in this town. There are souks of every kind in Deira and you would be hard put not to find something of interest. Shopping expeditions are even more fun at night. Dull lanes become transformed into dazzling labyrinths filled with crowds of bargain hunters and the riotous sound of fevered deal-making. The narrow corridors of the spice souk are especially enjoyable to walk along, but there are also perfume, textiles, leather, clothes, vegetable and fish souks. The most famous one, of course, is the **gold souk**, where, in its hundreds of little shops, all that glitters is definitely gold. For the best electrical goods, take a look around Baniyas Square at the Al-Sabkha Road end.

On the Dubai side, near to where the abras dock, is the **Old Souk**, which is less frenetic than its Deira counterparts, but atmospheric nonetheless. Next to it is the imposing **Ruler's Office**, with decorative traditional rooftop windtowers. But 51 for the genuine "old" Dubai, carry on a short distance along the Creek to the **Bastakiya** district. These buildings dating from around the first decade of the 20th century were once merchants' houses. The square windtowers were an early form of air-conditioning and their open vents funnelled any available breeze into the rooms below. Bastakiya is now a prized conservation area.

The adjacent **Al-Fahidi Fort**, constructed in the early 1800s, originally served to protect the Creek from foreign invaders. It has acted as both palace to the ruling sheikhs and Dubai's seat of government. Since 1971 it has housed the **Dubai Museum**. In the courtyard is a *barasti*, or reed house. These houses were common throughout the region up to the 1950s. An excellent exhibition showing Dubai's history from the 1930s onwards has been installed beneath the fort. There is an extensive waxwork display of life in the 1950s, useful information on Arabian essentials such as wildlife in the desert, the role of the camel, national costume, a timely reminder of the contribution of Arabs to astronomy and navigation, and the chance to see inside a Bedouin black tent. There is an interesting archaeological display at the end of the museum. Look out for two particularly striking exhibits, a pair of graves from the Qusais tombs, three to four thousand years old. The Al-Qusais site, 13 km (8 miles) northeast of Dubai, is open to the public.

A fine building in the traditional style, **Sheikh Saeed's House** near the mouth of the Creek was built in the late 19th century. Sheikh Saeed was the present ruler's grandfather and lived here until his death in 1958. An extensive renovation programme has carefully restored the house to its former glory. Made from coral stone, lime and plaster, it is classically proportioned with an inner courtyard and finely carved archways, doors and windows. The house now contains a museum of ancient documents.

Inevitably, Dubai's architecture goes well beyond the traditional. The Creek skyline is a remarkable mix of mosques, mansions, ferris wheels, high-rise hotels and post-modern skyscrapers—the building with what looks like a gigantic golfball on top is the Telecom Tower. For an unparalleled view of the whole rich confection, make the ascent to the roof of the 39-storey **World Trade Centre** (by guided tour only, twice daily at 9.30 a.m. and 4.30 p.m.). Look in the other direc-

Racing camels heading for the starting line. One of these fine beasts can cost as much as a hundred thousand dollars.

tion, however, and all you see is sand. In Arabia, the desert is never very far away.

A good example of modern Islamic architecture, something not always easy to locate in the hurly-burly of the emirate's building explosion, is the sand-coloured **Jumeirah Mosque** to the west of Dubai. This shows up especially well in the evening, when it is floodlit.

A favourite destination for visitors is the **camel racing**, which takes place on Thursdays and Fridays during the winter. Don't expect any mile classics;

the participants, with their un-hurried, loping style, take some time to get up a head of steam. The races start early, so aim at getting to the track by 8 a.m. Horse racing is equally popular. The emirate is home to the Dubai World Cup, the richest horse race in the world. Night meetings at the Dubai Racing Club are particularly atmospheric as well as pleasantly cool.

On most golf courses in Arabia, you have to carry around with you a small square of astroturf from which you tee off into a seemingly endless sand- 53 trap. But Dubai now boasts three championship-level grass courses. The **Dubai Creek Golf Club** is worth visiting just for the club house alone. Built in the image of the billowing sails of a dhow, it resembles more a scaled-down version of the Sydney Opera House. The courses are open to visitors and equipment can be hired, but it's a good idea to check first as to the best time to go.

As a break from the hectic whirl of metropolitan life in Dubai, take a trip out to the mountain village of **Hatta**. On the road to Hatta the sand turns deep red, as if burnt by the sun. In fact it's the effect of iron ore from the Hajar Mountains. The dunes are formed into waves by the northwest wind and grow higher and more crescent-shaped as they approach the mountain range. Excavations on the left side of the Juma valley near Hatta have revealed another ancient settlement similar to that at Umm an-Nar; 50 tombs were found dating from the 3rd millenium BC. Artefacts from these can be seen in the Dubai museum. The Hatta Heritage Village contains a restored 200-year-old settlement and gives access to the old Omani fort. The Juma Friday mosque situated scenically in a palm grove is also worth visiting.

Sharjah

Throughout the 19th century Sharjah had been Dubai's main trade rival, though its position was increasingly eclipsed by its neighbour's canny business manoeuvres. Nevertheless, it was here that the British chose to locate the first airport of any consideration in the Gulf when, in 1932, Imperial Airways began using it as a staging post for its Asian routes. In the 1950s it was the site of a Royal Air Force base and today it remains the UAE's biggest handler of air-cargo. The low point came in the 1950s and 60s. While Dubai's Creek was being dredged and improved, Sharjah's harbour was negligently allowed to silt up. And as oil-rich Abu Dhabi gained political ascendency among the emirates, Sharjah had to wait until 1972 for its first drop of oil to be discovered. The in-fighting among the ruling al-Qasimi family can't have helped much. There was an attempted coup in 1972 and the latest quarrel was only in 1987, when the ruler's brother tried to overthrow him. With the weight of the UAE's Supreme Council on his side though, Sheikh Sultan was soon restored to power.

As anyone looking at the city today can see, Sharjah has survived and flourished. Hoping

A turquoise mosque gleams in a forest of concrete.

to cash in on the overspill from Dubai's economic success, Sharjah underwent a massive hotel-building boom. Some were nervous about the huge over-capacity and feared a corresponding bust, but the city seems to keep on growing. The **Central Market**, or New Souk, is a manifestation of this optimism. A civic building project on the grand scale, it looks disconcertingly like a row of connected oriental "cathedrals" topped with blue domes and square towers. In fact these are working windtowers, which achieve a welcome degree of coolness inside. This is very much a modern shopping mall, and if your taste in souks runs more to the orderly than the riotous, this is the one to head for. It is also reputed to have some of

55

the best bargains in the Emirates. On the upper floors in particular, you can find a whole host of shops selling Persian carpets, silverware, jewellery and that symbol of gracious Arabian living, the long-necked coffee pot.

Across Al-Ittihad Square from the Central Market, the **King Faisal Mosque** counterbalances the more worldly attractions of the souk. As the largest mosque in the UAE, it can accommodate up to 3,000 worshippers at a time.

Rolla Square, just off lively Al-Arouba Road, Sharjah's main downtown street, is the favoured place to be when the sun goes down. On public holidays this is the scene of large celebratory parades, but usually it is just a relaxing place to hang out for a while with all the locals.

The **Old Souk**, towards the corniche, has been extensively restored. Although it now has the slightly cleaned-up air of a museum piece about it, its narrow, covered lanes are still a wonderful place to walk around for their atmospheric evocation of a past way of life in Arabia. The stores are inevitably aimed towards the tourist, with coin, jewellery and antique shops contending for the visitor's dirhams.

The Sharjah coast is dotted with picturesque old **watchtowers**, evidence of an earlier turbulent time when the al-Qasimi clan were a warlike naval power on the Gulf. A particularly romantic example stands alone on the sand bar which juts out opposite the main corniche. On the way there, a small island in the Khalid Lagoon offers turbulence of a different kind in the brightly lit **amusement park**. It is open every day except Saturday. Mondays are reserved for women and children only.

For an enjoyable excursion, head out on the Sharjah to Dhaid road to **Desert Park**, a gleaming new natural history museum intriguingly situated in the middle of nowhere. The museum makes excellent use of graphics, videos and models and throughout has an underlying ecological theme. You can walk on the sea bed in a "Living Seas" exhibition, take a journey through time in an exploration of the "Big Bang" onwards, and learn a great deal about the desert, stretching back to the earliest moments of the peninsula. Given the museum's location, it is unsurprising that it

Sharjah's minarets and Union Monument, reaching for the sky.

56

should be an important subject here. But it's strange to reflect that Arabia was once like the African savannah, covered by lush jungle and supporting animals such as zebras and hippos. Also look out for what should by now be a familiar section in the UAE's museums—a gallery of photographs showing the remarkable transformation of the emirate in question. In this case, there are some good aerial pictures of Sharjah from 1935 to the present day.

Dhaid, an oasis town 50 km (31 miles) east of Sharjah city, was once the place where the emirate's wealthy went to escape the heat. The advent of air-conditioning has ended the need for such drastic action, but the town still looks very inviting on a hot day. Set in a hollow, the green of the oasis, with two brilliant white minarets protruding from within, appears suddenly as you come over the rise of the hill. Dhaid itself is a fairly quiet town. The new souk will be familiar as it is a dowdier version of Sharjah's, a design that has clearly proved a big success in this emirate.

Ajman

Ajman is the smallest of the seven emirates, a mere 260 sq km (100 sq miles) in area. The first recognition that this tiny settlement was an independent sheikhdom came in 1820 when the British forced the ruler to sign the General Treaty of Peace along with all the other Gulf leaders. Since then it has managed to carve out an identity for itself as a famous dhow-building centre—even today the boatyards along the waterfront are a popular destination for visitors wishing to see the old skills still in use. Ajman has not been blessed with any oil discoveries but has benefited from being part of a federation where revenues from oil, primarily from Abu Dhabi's vast fields, are used to support poorer states. Its enclave at Musfut in the Hajar Mountains, however, yields high-grade marble as well as a vital resource for modern tourism, mineral water.

Ajman's well-preserved **fort** should not be missed. It is one of the finest old forts along the Gulf and also contains a good museum. Built in the second half of the 18th century, it reflects a mixture of architectural styles, from the Portuguese-influenced Arabian bastions to the traditional Arabian wind towers. Ajman's rulers lived here until 1970 when it became the local police headquarters. In 1981 the new ruler, Humaid V, gave instructions for it to be converted into a **museum** dedicated to

Ajman's cultural heritage. In the forecourt there are a couple of examples of the traditional boats built in Ajman, including a *sam'aa*, or pearling dhow, plus an old-style palm-branch house which looks rather comfortable inside. The museum shop on the left as you enter sells local handicrafts as well as a useful museum guide.

The museum has gone into waxwork displays in a big way. They are used to demonstrate costumes, women's crafts, children's games and the old-style kitchen, and one long room is given over to a reconstruction of a typical street in the old souk. There is an excellent collection of photographs of famous Ajmani pearl divers, whose exploits are recorded for posterity. And not to be missed is the chance to actually sit beneath a windtower and test whether they really work. Reflecting its previous incarnation, the museum also has a police exhibition with such unusual displays as a wooden punishment block, police pistols, manacles and tear-gas bombs.

If you don't mind an early start, it is worth seeing the food **souks** on the waterfront. The

---

Mapping by camel

Manama is an oasis town on the Dhaid road from Sharjah to the east coast. It is a quiet spot, containing an old fort which functions as a police station, and a red fort which is an army base. It is probably wise not to photograph either of them. The town is an Ajmani enclave in what might seem more naturally to be part of Sharjah. This apparent anomaly is due to the complicated map drawn up by a British Foreign Office agent, who roamed the interior by camel in the 1950s. As a result, parcels of one emirate often appear in another one. A Sharjah enclave on the east coast divides Fujairah in two, and it is impossible to get from one side to the other without entering Sharjah territory. Indeed, further along the Fujairah coast, there is a road that welcomes you to Oman. This is a small circle of land that is entirely surrounded by the UAE and would seem to have no good reason to be part of another country. Of course, the British cartographer's main task had more to with ensuring that each Sheikh felt sufficiently content with the amount of land he received, than it had to do with logic. The hope was that it would stifle long-lasting resentment, although this hasn't always been the outcome. As recently as 1972, Sharjah and Fujairah were fighting—quite violently at times—over their borders.

59

fish souk is particularly lively and at its best before 8 a.m. when the fishermen have just brought in the day's catch. Not far away is where they dock their boats. These line the jetty and, covered in their complicated web of fishing nets, look very photogenic.

Umm al-Qaiwain

The little fishing village of Umm al-Qaiwain was built on the tip of a thin spit of land which protrudes from the Gulf coastline like a crooked finger. In the past, an important source of income for the emirate was the manufacture and sale of brightly coloured postage stamps. One couldn't post anything with them, though, as they were purely for philatelists with a taste for the exotic. Today, despite the staggering changes that the oil years have brought to the region, Umm al-Qaiwain remains a sleepy, relatively undeveloped place where you will see goats being herded through the main street and the skyscraper is unknown. This lends it considerable charm, for it is the nearest experience to what life was like in the emirates before the oil boom.

Things haven't always been so quiet. The **old fort**, dating from the 17th century, was bombarded by the British as part of their punitive raid on the Pirate Coast. It is as picturesque as any of the Gulf forts, with a row of cannons outside looking suitably martial, but unfortunately it is not open to the public.

The nearby **mosque** was built in the 19th century on an unusual open plan. The Arabic date over the doorway says 1286 AH—year One of the Islamic calendar began in AD 622 after the *hijrah* (migration), when Mohammed fled from Mecca to escape a murder plot.

Umm al-Qaiwain is a good place to find more of the northern Gulf's old watchtowers. Fishing is still a major part of the economy, and the emirate is an important supplier to the whole of the UAE. Walk along the beach and you will soon encounter fishermen either returning with their catch or hanging up rows of fishing nets to dry.

Ras al-Khaimah

Like many other parts of the UAE, archaeological excavations have revealed early settlements in Ras al-Khaimah going back at least 5,000 years. But even its recorded history is a long and rich one. The origins of the city lie a few kilometres north in the ancient town of Julfar, which was a major port as far back as the 7th century and involved in a trade network that stretched to India and China. The Portuguese explorer Vasco da Gama arrived there in 1498 en route to India. He was helped by the famous Arabic navigator, Ahmed bin Majid, who came from Ras al-Khaimah and led da Gama to Calicut. Ironically, by so doing, he also assured Portuguese control of the lucrative oriental spice trade and guaranteed its ascendency over Ras al-Khaimah for the next 100 years. During the 16th century the Portuguese built a customs house and fort and generally ran the show. By the early 1600s though, the trade-hungry British and Dutch were in the region. Together with local tribes they attacked Julfar, pushing out the Portuguese and destroying their buildings. Julfar was abandoned by its Arab inhabitants in 1633 when they moved to modern Ras Al-Khaimah city.

The Al-Qasimi tribe established themselves as rulers here in 1747 (and later in Sharjah as well), controlling the Straits of Hormuz and repelling colonial powers. At the beginning of the 19th century they had a fleet of over 850 ships manned by 19,000 men. This threat to British power led to the decisive 1820 invasion and signing of the Peace Treaty between the defeated sheikhdoms and Britain. When the UAE was formed in 1971, Ras al-Khaimah initially declined to join the federation, taking a further two months to acknowledge the inevitable.

The emirate is one of the most beautiful in the UAE, with spectacular mountain scenery and coastline. It is also very fertile, producing a large percentage of the country's food requirements and earning a name as the breadbasket of the nation. After many years' prospecting, oil was discovered in commercial quantities in 1983 and Ras al-Khaimah became the fourth contributor to the UAE's fuel bonanza.

The city is divided by a lagoon, with the old town situated on the western side. Here, in Ras al-Khaimah fort, is another excellent **museum**. The fort was built by the Persians during their brief period of rule in the early part of the 18th century. Most of what you see today, however, is no more than 100 years old, rebuilt after it was heavily bombed by the British in 1820. The museum is particularly informative on the emirate's archaeological sites and its natural history. There's a fine display of Bedouin silver jewellery and an excellent coin collection. In 1985, a local farmhand found more than 120 coins while he was digging a well. 61

They turned out to be 11th-century silver dirhams struck at the Oman mint at Sohar. Take time to look at the Qawasim Room, whose raison d'être is to refute Britain's description of the area as the Pirate Coast. Defending their ancestors' good name, the modern Al-Qawasim (Qawasim being the plural of Qasimi) assert that the British raids had less to do with quelling piracy than maintaining Britain's monopoly of maritime trade. On the upper floor there's another chance to test the effectiveness of a windtower.

The old town's **souk**, not far from the museum, is worth a visit for its easy-going atmosphere, but bear in mind that in Ras al-Khaimah, as in Saudi Arabia, the shops shut at prayer times.

There are a number of interesting places to see outside the emirate's main city, although you'll require some perseverance reach to them. Some 5 km (3 miles) to the north are the excavations at **Shimal**. Known locally as Qasr az-Zubba, Sheba's Palace, these early hilltop fortifications and buildings, which overlie a pre-Islamic stronghold, have as much to do with the famous queen as one of the UAE's new 5-star hotels (she was from Yemen, in fact). However, they do suggest the presence of a powerful military force here long before the rise of Julfar in the 7th century and were still in use as recently as the 1500s. The hill is quite steep but the view from the top is well worth the effort.

A few kilometres north, **Rams** is where the British marines landed in 1819. A quiet seaside village, it has a very pleasant harbour which is nice for a stroll. You can't miss the old watchtowers, one of which is in the centre of the village. They obviously served their purpose—as the British came ashore the population of Rams fled north to the fort at **Dhayah**. This is set back from the coast on a hilltop covered in sea shells, so the climb up is slippery and calls for caution. It is remarkable to think that once, before the peninsula began to heat up after the last Ice Age, these mountains were under water. Dhayah has the distinction of being the last Qawasim stronghold to be taken by the British before this area became "trucial".

If all the hill-climbing proves too exhausting, head south inland from Ras al-Khaimah to the **Khatt Hot Springs**. It's not difficult to relax here in the warm mineral waters and enjoy the friendly atmosphere engendered among the bathers. There

Badiyah mosque in Fujairah claims to be the oldest in all the Emirates.

are separate pools for men and women.

The emirate also has one of the country's best camel racing tracks. At Digdagga, 10 km (6 miles) south of the capital, the pace can get very hot, although this usually has more to do with the reactions of the crowd than the speed of the racers.

Fujairah

Fujairah lies entirely on the Batinah, or east coast, and is thus the only emirate without a presence on the Arabian Gulf. To compensate, it has the most spectacular scenery in the UAE—the road north from Fujairah to Dibba compares with any of the world's great coastal drives, running between the stark, volcanic Hajar mountains and the beautiful beaches of the Gulf of Oman. Throughout the 19th century Fujairah was considered to be part of Sharjah. It wasn't until 1952 that the British government recognized it as a separate 63 sheikhdom. Due to the eccentric arrangement of the emirates' borders however, Sharjah still rules the port of Khor Fakkan, neatly splitting Fujairah in two.

Fujairah is a quiet, unspoilt town with a fine corniche on which to enjoy the late afternoon breeze. Its purpose-built **museum** opened in 1991 and has an especially strong archaeological section. There are certainly plenty of ancient sites in the area for it to concentrate on, and you can see potsherds, axes and vessels from excavations at the 4,500-year-old tombs at Bidya (Badiyah), as well as artefacts from Bithna and Qidfa, including a container made from an ostrich egg.

The 300-year-old **fort**, a little way out from the town, is a brooding ruin that presides over the crumbling mud walls of a deserted village. The fort was shelled by the British in 1825, with the intention of securing the release of the sheikh's slaves.

South of Fujairah, **Khor Kalba** has Arabia's oldest black mangrove forest and is a must for bird-watchers.

The best archaeological site to visit is at **Bithna** in the Hajar

Fishing boats at anchor in Khor Fakkan.

mountains. Beneath a corrugated iron awning is the Iron Age T-shaped tomb, a communal burial chamber discovered in 1988. The Fujairah museum has useful information on this site. Also at Bithna, an old fort provides good views across the mountain pass which it once guarded.

Going north along the coast, **Khor Fakkan** is known for its magnificent sandy beach, but there is also an attractive whitewashed mosque by the waterfront. This town is an increasingly popular tourist destination for UAE residents, although the beach's scenic beauty has been somewhat impaired by the development of a large container port at one end and the circular Oceanic Hotel at the other.

Next to the main road at **Badiyah** you can see a small, four-domed mosque, claimed as the oldest in the UAE. In the hills behind it are the ruins of more old watchtowers.

Carry on to **Dibba** at the Oman border and you will be treated to a spectacular view of the Musandam headland, which stretches up to the Straits of Hormuz. Dibba is a landmark for Islam in Arabia: following the victory of Muslim armies over local tribesmen in AD 633, just one year after Mohammed's death, Islam could claim control over the entire Arabian peninsula. Nowadays, Dibba is a peaceful and very picturesque seaside town which amply repays the traveller's endeavours to get there.

Eating Out

There is little that might be called an indigenous UAE cuisine. The nomadic Bedouin had a limited diet: on special occasions they might feast on goat or mutton with rice but the staple was camel's milk and dates, known as "the mother and the aunt of the Arabs". The coastal Arabs, of course, had a supply of fish to vary their meals. What we know as Middle Eastern cuisine mainly comprises Lebanese, Iranian and Moroccan, all of which are readily available throughout the Emirates. For the less adventurous, all types of Western cooking can also be found, from hamburgers to the English Sunday lunch. Given Dubai's large population of workers from the sub-continent, it is no surprise that several good Indian restaurants are to be found there.

The best way to sample a range of Arabian specialities is to order a *mezze*, a Middle Eastern smorgasbord of starters that is as filling as a main course. On one tray you will be introduced 65

Succulent dates of every size and shade.

to such delights as *tabbouleh* (cracked wheat salad with tomatoes, mint and parsley), *hummus* (a chick pea and sesame seed purée), *moutabel* (a delicious aubergine purée), *wara einab* (stuffed vine leaves with rice), and *tahini* (a dip of sesame seed paste, yoghurt and lemon). If you are still able, try a main dish such as *makbous* (spiced lamb with rice), *hareis* (long-simmered wheat and tender lamb), *meshwi* (a mixed grill of various types of meat and sausage), or any of the locally caught fish or shellfish such as red snapper, kingfish, pomfret, lobster and crab. A traditional snack is *shawarma* (grilled slivers of chicken or lamb, served with salad and stuffed into a pita bread). This is universally available at small shops and stands and is better known in the West via its incarnation as the doner kebab.

Popular desserts include *esh asaraya* (a type of cheesecake) and *umm'ali* (bread pudding with cinnamon and nutmeg), which some in the region have mischievously suggested was introduced by a Miss O'Malley, an Irish mistress of the Khedive Ismail. The Middle East is

66

famous for its sweet tooth and even sweeter pastries, although fruit is the usual conclusion to a meal. The most common, of course, are dates, which grow throughout the more fertile areas of the UAE and at times have been responsible for the survival of the Bedouin.

Coffee is more than just a drink, it is an expression of the culture. Business and bargaining are traditionally never done without it, and coffee houses are repositories of cordiality and conversation (and, typically, only men). Roasted and pulverized beans are brewed in small brass coffee pots and served in tiny cups. The sugar is usually boiled at the same time and the coffee will be very sweet unless you make it clear you want it either *mazbout* (medium sweet) or *murra* (unsweetened). Don't stir the coffee, and let the grounds settle before drinking.

Remember, Muslim dietary laws apply. This means that in most places a sandwich and a beer won't be an option at lunchtime. Fortunately, the UAE being a relatively liberal society, you can obtain pretty much anything your taste buds fancy at the big Western hotel restaurants and bars. Prices for alcohol can be pretty steep, however. Sharjah is an exception to this and bans all alcohol.

Shopping

As almost all the emirates operate as open ports with low import duties, goods from around the world appear in the shops and the souks at enticing bargain prices. At times it seems that the UAE is a vast Aladdin's cave crammed with the very latest watches, cameras, camcorders, fashion and textiles, perfumes and cosmetics. There will be plenty to tempt even the least enthusiastic shopper, but don't take the first price you're offered—bargaining is expected. The main thing is to enjoy the experience, for shopping here is something that engages all the senses.

There's no need to settle just for the high-tech and the modern, though. As one might expect given its location and its culture, the UAE is a great place to buy traditional goods from the Middle East. Sharjah and Dubai are known for their excellent prices on Persian carpets (but US Customs bans their importation). Other popular items include antique silver jewellery, Marie-Therese dollars (until recently an accepted local currency), brass coffee sets, hand-carved wooden dhow models and various ornaments set with turquoise, lapis lazuli and other semi-precious stones. 67

Practical Information

Business hours. Banks: 8 a.m. to noon, Saturday to Thursday (Thursday to 11 a.m. in Abu Dhabi). Shops: with variations, 9 a.m. to 1 p.m. and 4 p.m. to 9 p.m. or later, Saturday to Thursday. Souks open Friday as well.

Climate. Average summer temperatures (Apr–Sept): days 40°C (104°F), nights 32°C (90°F); East coast and mountain regions cooler. In winter months, more temperate, with desert areas becoming cold at night.

Clothing. Lightweight clothing for daytime throughout the year, with sweater or jacket needed for winter evenings. Conservative dress in public is advisable. Except for poolside, women should avoid wearing tight or revealing clothing. Sunhat, sunglasses and sun block cream are essential.

Currency. The *dirham* (Dh) is divided into 100 *fils*. Coins from 1 fils to Dh 5. Notes from Dh 5 to Dh 500. Old and new coins are equally valid, but some public telephones and vending machines have not yet been converted to accept the new coins.

Electricity. In Abu Dhabi: 220/240 V AC, 50 Hz. In the northern states, 220 V AC, 50 Hz. Plugs have 3 square pins.

Language. Arabic, with English widely understood.

Photography. Be sensitive about photographing local people, especially women. You should not take photos of airports, government buildings or military subjects.

Religion. Predominantly Sunni Muslim, with minorities of Ibadi and Shiite Muslims. During the holy month of Ramadan, Muslims fast and refrain from smoking between sunrise and sunset. Tourists should be considerate and not eat or smoke in public. Dates of Ramadan change yearly.

Telephone. Calls within each state are free. The country code is 971. To make an international call, dial 00 then the country code, the area code and local number.

Time difference. GMT + 4.

OMAN

Fortresses and Frankincense

The Arabia of myth and legend lives on in Oman: desert forts guarded by white-robed figures armed with ancient rifles and curved daggers; palm-shaded oases; the home port of Sindbad the Sailor; and a fiercely independent but hospitable, courteous people. And yes, oil, although in modest quantities so that the income has permitted sensible development but little in the way of extravagance.

Lying along the eastern shores of the Arabian peninsula, Oman covers some 300,000 sq km (115,000 sq miles). At the far northern tip, and cut off from the rest, is the Musandam Peninsula, a beak of land pushing out into the Strait of Hormuz and occupying a strategic position overlooking the entry to the Arabian Gulf.

The coastline is at its most inviting around Salalah on the Arabian Sea in the south, and in the north between Shinas and Mutrah where it is known as the Batinah. Long, lovely beaches, feathery date palms, groves of citrus and lush fields of alfalfa embellish this curving fertile plain, backed by the towering Hajar mountains, whose peaks climb to more than 3,000 m (10,000 ft). Beyond this stone wall, the land falls away again into the endless spaces of the Arabian Desert.

Unlike the people of the interior, whose isolation made them self-reliant and aloof, the coastal dwellers have had centuries of contact with the outside world. Their ancestors sailed before the monsoon winds to trade with India and East Africa, and they carry the traces of Asian intermarriage to this day. The people are mainly cultivators, herdsmen or fishermen, some of them still putting to sea in curious rafts of palm wood. Their traditional palm houses, *barasti*, built so as to get the full benefit of any sea breeze, are now mainly museum pieces, though you may spot one or two along the coast.

The Green Mountain (Jebel Akhdar), so called from the colour of the rock, is a cool, craggy highland dotted with orange orchards, vineyards and walnut groves, with natural areas where flowers run riot—roses, marigolds and tall pink hollyhocks. In Saiq, a town of roses, the petals are collected and boiled, and the liquid distilled to make rosewater, on sale throughout the country.

Inland oases support fig, peach, apricot and pomegranate trees. Water to irrigate them is

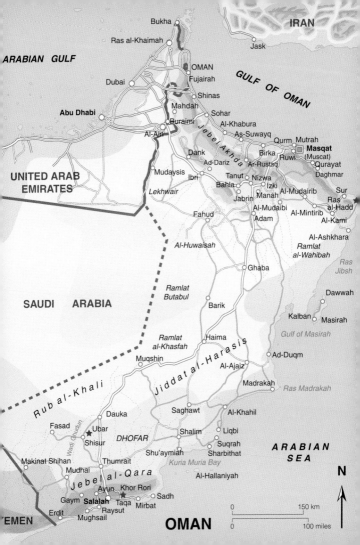

brought from the mountains by the age-old *falaj* system of tunnels and stone channels. The supply is extremely reliable, even over long dry spells.

The west and centre of the country is a sun-beaten land of shifting sand dunes and thorn bushes, habitable only by a few Bedouin, their camels and goats, and in recent years, oilmen. Animals in the more remote regions include the shy Arabian tahr, a kind of gazelle, panthers, wild cats, wolves, porcupines and rare black hedgehogs. The seas are exceptionally rich in fish, and the government is concerned to protect stocks from foreign fleets which would over-exploit them.

South is the province of Dhofar, with another beautiful coastal plain, hemmed in by the rugged Jebel al-Qara. The often generous rainfall of the summer monsoons brings a rush of new growth, dressing the hillsides in verdant green, to the surprise of first-time visitors who come expecting desert.

Frankincense, the fabled scent borne by the Three Kings, was Dhofar's most famous export for thousands of years and was even sent to the Great Temple

---

Rebirth of a Nation

A major sea power in the Middle Ages, later a great trading empire and the first Arab state to send an ambassador to the United States, Oman had, by the mid-20th century, become an isolated backwater. Racked by internal squabbles, desperately poor, it was cut off from the outside world by its ruler, Sultan Said bin Taimur, who was dead set against development of any kind. He banned travel abroad, and severely restricted it even within Oman. His son Qaboos bin Said was allowed to go to Britain for his education but on returning home was put under virtual house arrest. When oil revenues began to flow in during the 1960s, Said refused to spend them to improve the lot of his people.

In 1970, Qaboos took over power in a bloodless coup and immediately began to make up for lost time. Within a few years, hospital beds increased from a mere 12 to over 3,000, and the number of children in school went from 900 to a quarter of a million (primarly enrolment is now over 80 per cent). Then, there were only 10 km (6 miles) of paved road in the whole country; now there are thousands, including 1,100 km (680 miles) of highway from Muscat to Salalah. Amid all this change, traditional ways of life have been remarkably preserved, and the country is more united than at any time in its history.

of Babylon. Salalah is the provincial capital, with a varied mix of people including many black Omanis, the descendants of immigrants from Zanzibar.

Oman's population of around 2 million is growing fast, now that infant mortality has been cut to a tiny fraction of the levels of thirty years ago. The language is Arabic, in several different dialects. Religion is almost 100 per cent Muslim, most people belonging to the Ibadhi sect which established its separate identity as early as the 7th century. In recent years there has been a cautious opening up to tourism and visitors have been given the chance to discover this friendly, fascinating corner of Arabia.

A Brief History

8000 BC	The area is inhabited by primitive hunters.
2000 BC	Agriculture develops on the coastal plain and in sheltered valleys, sustained by the *falaj* system of irrigation.
2nd century BC	Oman is already a trading and maritime centre for boats sailing to India, East Africa and even China. The frankincense trade brings wealth to the Dhofar region.
7th century AD	The Omanis are converted to Islam before the death of the Prophet Mohammed in 632. The Ibadhi sect takes the predominant role and imams are elected as religious and national rulers.
14th century	By now Sohar is a major port, rich and cosmopolitan through its imports from the East.
16th century	In 1507 a Portuguese fleet commanded by Alfonso de Albuquerque arrives off the coast, capturing Muscat, Sohar and other ports, to protect their sea routes to India and the Spice Islands of Indonesia.
17th century	Civil war between rival leaders ends when Nasir bin Murshid is elected Imam. He unites the country between 1624 and 1649 and starts evicting the Portuguese from their coastal strongholds. Sultan bin Saif succeeds his cousin in 1650. The Portuguese are finally driven out, irrigation systems are repaired, agriculture extended and the navy improved until it even chases the Portuguese to India.

73

18th century	Oman takes the island of Zanzibar, off the east coast of Africa, in 1730. Civil war caused by internal rivalry ends with the election of Ahmad bin Said as imam in 1749. In 1785 the roles of imam and sultan are divided between his two sons. Britain is concerned about possible French intervention in the area, and in 1798 signs the first of a series of agreements with Oman, guaranteeing to protect it against aggressors.
19th century	Under Sultan Said bin Sultan, known as Said the Great, who rules from 1804 to 1856, the Omani empire thrives. Said adds Dhofar to his realm and controls part of the East African coast, together with ports in Persia and Baluchistan. Upon his death, one of his sons becomes Sultan of Zanzibar, another the Sultan of Muscat and Oman. Britain persuades the new sultan to end trade in slaves and arms, resulting in a great drop in revenues. Led by the imam, the interior rises up against the sultan's rule.
20th century	On the death of Sultan Faisal bin Turki in 1913, the tribes of the interior refuse to accept his son Taimur bin Faisal as ruler. They attack Muscat but are repelled, with British assistance. An uneasy peace is reached between the sultan and the imam in 1920 with the Treaty of Seeb.

Sultan Said bin Taimur succeeds his father in 1938 and embarks on a policy of isolation from the rest of the world, rejecting all forms of modernization. In the 1950s he moves to take over most of the interior. Revolts are suppressed and peace is achieved, again with British help, in 1959. A long-running border dispute over the ownership of the Buraimi Oasis is settled. Rebellion erupts again in 1963 in the southern province of Dhofar.

Oil is discovered in central Oman; exports begin in 1967, but Sultan Said lacks the vision to make good use of the revenues. In 1970, Sultan Qaboos bin Said deposes his father and moves rapidly to improve education, health care, communications and living standards. The Dhofar war finally ends in 1976. Oil output diminishes but prospecting continues, along with steady agricultural and industrial expansion, and a limited development of tourism.

Many southern Omanis are descendants of immigrants from Zanzibar.   75

The Capital Area

Greater Muscat is made up of three distinct cities, separated geographically by hills and ridges, and each with its own particular identity. Muscat is the old port area; Mutrah, to the northwest, is the main trading district with the country's most important harbour; whereas Ruwi, built on a grid-plan in a valley a few kilometres inland, has developed only in the late 20th century into a modern commercial and administrative centre. Still newer appendages are the largely residential suburb of Qurm, and Medinat Qaboos with many government buildings, west of Mutrah on the coast. Al-Bustani, south of Muscat, boasts a luxury hotel.

Muscat

For centuries, visiting seamen have painted or cut the names of their ships on the cliffs which tumble to the sea at Muscat. The word *masquat* means "place of falling", and refers to these precipitous rocks. Nor was Nelson himself too proud to add his own contribution when he came here as a young midshipman. These same rough black hills have allowed Oman's chief city to keep one of its claims to fame: that of being the smallest capital in the world—or so the Omanis say. At one time you could get here only by sea, but today a coast road links Muscat and Mutrah.

Muscat has been the capital since the sultans of the Al-Bu Said dynasty chose it as their residence towards the end of the 18th century. It's a walled town with four **gates**, used nowadays to regulate the traffic. The main gate, Bab al-Kabir, serves incoming vehicles, which leave by Bab al-Waljat. Bab al-Mathaib is reserved for heavy traffic and Bab al-Saghir for pedestrians and donkeys. Though there is little in the way of "tourist attractions" in the old city, most people love wandering around its steep, narrow streets to soak up the traditional atmosphere. Walk through the main gate to Wadi al-Kabir. Further on is an old graveyard and further still, you come to **Tawiyan al-Alwiyat**, Place of Wells. One is still worked by bullocks.

The city is guarded east and west by two great stone forts, built on Arab foundations by the Portuguese in the late 16th century, making the port almost impregnable. Until the 1970s,

Non-Muslims can admire the elegance of this gold-domed mosque, but only from outside.

cannons were fired from the two towers every night as the town gates were dragged shut. Both forts are used by the police and army and are closed to the public, though you can take photos. **Fort Jalali**, to the east, used to serve as a prison. The Sultan's Royal Guard is installed in **Fort Mirani**, where there are still some old bronze cannons.

The Sultan's imposing **palace** stands on the waterfront. You will see fine Omani houses in a combination of Arab, Indian and Portuguese styles, with beautifully carved doors and high walls at least 3 ft thick, to keep out the heat. Here and there, pink or purple bougainvillaea makes a brilliant splash against the blinding white walls. Among the most attractive of

Sailing to America

Sultan Said bin Sultan, ruler of Oman and Zanzibar, wanted to extend Omani commerce far beyond the shores of the Indian Ocean. In 1833, he signed a treaty with the United States to establish diplomatic and trade links. Determined that it should be more than just a piece of paper, he resolved to send a ship all the way to New York. The three-masted sailing ship *Sultanah* was prepared for the epic voyage. She left Muscat on December 23, 1839, carrying the sultan's emissary with letters and gifts for President Van Buren, including two fine Arabian horses, pearls, a Persian carpet and a gold-mounted sword. The general cargo included dates, coffee, spices and hides. After calling at Zanzibar to pick up cloves and ivory, the *Sultanah* rounded the Cape of Good Hope, called in at St Helena, then headed for New York. Her arrival on April 30, 1840 created a sensation; the crew were feted and taken on city tours and train rides. The goods were quickly sold and for the journey home, muskets, music boxes, mirrors, china and glass, lamps and chandeliers were bought. Return presents for the sultan included rifles inscribed "From the President of the United States to the Imam of Muscat".

    Sultanah sailed for home on August 9, 1840 and reached Zanzibar on December 8, calling only at Cape Town to break the arduous voyage. Sadly, no permanent trade links were forged, and no ship from Oman visited a US port for the next 146 years. Then, as part of the centenary celebrations for the Statue of Liberty, the sail training ship *Shabab Oman* repeated the journey of her predecessor to join a "tall ships" parade in New York.

Mutrah Fort looks as though it has grown out of the hill top.

these houses is **Beit Fransa** (once the French embassy and now a museum) near the main gate. **Beit Nadir**, built in the 18th century, is also a museum; it is situated on the main road.

Mutrah

Although it's also surrounded by hills, Mutrah has more room for expansion than Muscat. Recent development is apparent along the curving seaside road (the "Corniche"), where modern banks and offices alternate with old Omani and Indian-style houses. Ships dock at the modern port of **Mina Qaboos**, busy with a mixture of passenger and cargo vessels and time-worn wooden dhows.

Mutrah Fort, built entirely by the Portuguese in the 1580s, sits stolidly on a hilltop dominating the bay.

The main attraction for visitors is **Mutrah Souk**, full of rich fabrics from India, antiques and pottery, with heaps of colourful fruit and spices. Some of the most popular shops with foreign and local visitors alike are those specializing in silver jewellery. Enter the souk by the 79 main gateway on the coast road, take the first alleyway to the right and you'll find the silver traders beyond some fabric shops.

Mutrah is proud of its new fishery complex, but the old **fish market** on the dhow harbour is still going strong. The market opens at 6.30 a.m.; early morning is the best time to visit. Shell merchants also set up stalls here.

You can take a **boat tour** of the harbours and bays for the view of Muscat which greeted every visitor until recent times —from the sea. Some excursion boats can take you on trips along the coast for swimming, snorkelling and other water sports, landing at one of the idyllic beaches and even providing a picnic or barbecue lunch.

Ruwi

Many of the essential services that couldn't be squeezed into Mutrah or Muscat are located in Ruwi, and the streets are thronged with an extraordinary medley of nationalities.

Ruwi's hotels have become convenient meeting-places for business people, and several little restaurants have sprung up to cater for this transient, cosmopolitan population.

The whitewashed fort **Beit al-Falaj**, north of the town centre, was built in the late 18th century as a summer residence for the sultan. Set amid steep mountain slopes, it controlled the access to the valleys leading to Muscat. In a famous action in 1915, a handful of defenders held out against a force of thousands of rebellious tribesmen. Serving as the armed forces' headquarters until 1978, it has been transformed into the **Sultan's Armed Forces Museum**, run by the Omani army. With its fine carved doors and painted ceilings, the fortress-palace is an impressive setting for displays that trace Oman's history from pre-Islamic times to the recent past, including the defeat of the Jebel Akhdar and Dhofar insurrections. You'll be shown around by a guide.

There is a **souk** in Ruwi but it is modern and cannot compare with that of Mutrah. Ruwi clock tower is a landmark, especially at night when one side of it lights up as a "video-wall" of television screens.

Al-Bustan

A gently curving bay rimmed by a beach of golden sand, 6 km (4 miles) south of Muscat, or 9 km (6 miles) from Ruwi, was chosen as the site for the first meeting of the Gulf Cooperation Council (GCC) to be held in Oman. in 1985. To host the

Fishing by seine net close to the shore.

Gulf nations' rulers and their entourages, a spectacular palace and convention centre was built in arabesque style. After the conference, it was turned to good use as a luxury hotel, the **Al-Bustan Palace**. Even if you are not staying there, it's worth a visit; it may be possible to take a tour of some of the halls and rooms.

Qurm

West along the coast, 6 km (4 miles) from Mutrah, Qurm is a former fishing village which has come up in the world, providing a modern residential area for Greater Muscat. Among the government ministries in the **Medinat Qaboos** quarter on the western edge of Qurm, three museums are well worth visit-

81

ing if you want to learn more about Oman.

Exhibits in the **Oman Museum** (National Museum) cover the history, architecture and culture of the country, and there's also a display of local arts and crafts. Admission is free, and there's a free guidebook in English. The museum is housed in a small white building next to the Ministry of Information.

The **Children's Museum**, near the Foreign Ministry, has hands-on scientific displays that will interest grown-ups, too. Oman's geography, geology, flora and fauna can be examined in the **Natural History Museum**. Displays describe the efforts being made to protect Oman's wildlife, so beautifully adapted to the often harsh conditions but threatened by

Holding the Fort

Oman's history is written in the stone and mud-brick of its defensive architecture, from the great bastions that guard the coast to the chains of watch-towers that stand like broken teeth on almost every hilltop. Most evocative of all are the historic cities of the interior, former strongholds and palaces of imams and sultans at the edge of the desert. You can spend days exploring some of Oman's hundreds of monuments, many of them now restored or in the process of conservation, using traditional materials and techniques.

Because the two most prominent, the twin sentinels of Jalali and Mirani protecting Muscat Bay, were built by the Portuguese, many others have wrongly been attributed to them. In fact, only a few coastal forts are of Portuguese origin: the vast majority are the work of the Omani Ya'ariba dynasty which expelled the invaders in the 17th century, and the Al-Bu Said dynasty (that of the present sultan). Many, of course, stand on much older foundations; some dating from the 7th-century Sassanian empire ruled from Persia.

Omani forts are guarded by massive carved wooden portals, with a small cut-out door that admits only one stooping visitor at a time. A slot over the gateway allowed attackers to be drenched with boiling oil or something even nastier, a sticky, superheated brew made from dates! Inside, ceilings are usually of palm trunks supporting palm ribs and mats. State rooms have ceilings of candlewood, often painted with floral and geometric designs. North-facing windows let in cooling breezes while hot air escapes through small openings higher up. A fort invariably has a mosque, separate men's and women's living quarters, soldiers' rooms, prisons, stables for horses, food stores and water cisterns.

loss of habitat and human activities. A new attraction, since the dicovery af a whale skeleton, is the Whale Hall.

Two of the capital area's big international hotels are located near the sea west of Qurm, close to a long stretch of superb white sand beach. Between them, there's a small nature reserve where you can spot seabirds and waders, some of Oman's hundred or more species of birds.

Camel races are held on the old airstrip at **Seeb**. The camels, usually so aloof, actually look as though they are enjoying themselves, loping along with strange, rhythmic strides towards the finishing line, while young jockeys hang dangerously onto their backs.

Northern Oman

A convenient day trip west of the capital takes in coastal and mountain scenery, varied villages and a handful of historic sites.

The fort at **Barka**, on the coast 32 km (20 miles) west of Muscat has been restored to an almost too pristine state—it can surely never have looked this clean and perfect in all its history. An inscription records the name of Ahmad bin Said, 18th-century founder of the present Al-Bu Said dynasty and victor in Oman's last, decisive struggle to repel the Persians. Half-hidden among the palm trees behind Barka fort, **Beit Naman** is a fine example of a 17th-century fortified palace.

Inland at the foot of the mountains, warm springs bubble out of the ground at **Nakhl**. Its dramatically sited fortress perches on a precipice, following the contours of the rock so closely that it appears to grow from it. Restoration in recent years may have given it the look of a film set, but in fact the materials used are all authentic—the outside rendering is made from mud taken from local palm groves. From Nakhl's ramparts, on a clear day, you can just see Barka fort on the coast 40 km (25 miles) away.

Near the town of Awabi is the entrance to **Wadi Bani Kharus** which heads into the hills, winding past small villages which cling precariously to its rocky sides. A rugged four-wheel drive vehicle is essential for this (as for most wadi explorations), and it's a long and sometimes hair-raising drive to the end, but you are rewarded by superb views. Along the way, **Sital** is a picture-book village. An expert local guide will be able to show you ancient drawings on the rocks, depicting animal and hunting scenes.

83

Stylish date-seller complete with khanjar.

Rustaq served as the capital of Oman at various times during the Middle Ages and up to the early 18th century. Its fort, **Qalat al Kesra**, built over a natural spring, took many epochs to construct, starting with the Persian Sassanid Empire in the 7th century. The main structure dates from the Portuguese occupation, with later additions and extensive modern restoration. Climb up to the turrets for a wonderful view over the surrounding countryside. There is a small souk just outside the fort's entrance, at its most animated on Friday mornings.

Just off the road from Rustaq to the coast, only the brooding bulk of its fort suggests that the village of **Al-Hazm** was once an important centre. Although part of it dates from 1512, according to an inscription on an inner wall, most of the fortress was erected around 1710, the time of Sultan bin Saif II, fifth ruler of the Ya'ariba dynasty, who established his capital here. The depths of Al-Hazm guard his tomb and prayer cell, dark dungeons and, it's said, secret tunnels by which he could come and go. He is referred to in the carved inscription on the main right-hand door; that on the left-hand door bears the date 1162 AH (of the Hegira): around AD 1750.

One of the rooms upstairs constituted a mosque, as you'll gather from the *mihrab*, or prayer niche, cut into the wall, and there's also a Koranic school. In the room directly above the main entrance, note the holes through which visitors were examined, and through which hot oil was poured if they turned out to be unwelcome guests. On the roof you'll see some ancient cannon brought from Fort Mirani in Muscat and

---

Dressing in Style

Most Omani men wear a *dishdasha*, a long white gown of cotton or nowadays perhaps a synthetic fabric. Rank can only be guessed from the quality of the cloth and the accessories, a belt with a curved *khanjar* dagger, a turban or cap and, in cooler weather, a cloak or jacket. A man's turban is formed either from an embroidered Kashmiri square loosely wound, or of crisp white pleated cotton cleverly folded so that it keeps its shape even when taken off. But however handsome this headgear, it is the silver-embellished *khanjar* that catches the eye. Worn with justifiable pride, the finest examples are treasures of intricate filigree work on the sheaths and delicate chasing on the blades.

Women are seen in public far less than the menfolk. A stranger arriving in a village might glimpse no more than the end of a gown vanishing round a corner to suggest that the population is not exclusively male, or young, for children—boys and girls—are much in evidence. Women traditionally wear a voluminous outer dress or *abaya* over a tunic and trousers. Some, especially in rural areas, cover nose and mouth—sometimes the whole face—with a black mask or veil. Dhofari women's dress is more colourful, using velvets and bright silks, often gorgeously embroidered. Village children are the most vividly dressed of all, decked out in brilliant fabrics, with gaudy caps, anklets and bracelets and coloured cosmetics in their hair and around their bright eyes.

85

marked with the royal arms of Portugal. Water from an old *falaj* flows right into the fort, and also irrigates the gardens around it.

Nizwa

About 170 km (105 miles) from Muscat, the oasis town of Nizwa is an popular destination for day trips and—much better

---

Precious Waters: the *Falaj* System

You cannot travel far in Oman without noticing the beautifully designed stone channels which snake across the land, carrying water from distant springs and wells to villages and irrigating their gardens, palm groves and orchards. For thousands of years, life has depended on this complex system, known as *falaj*. To this day, no more efficient method has been found for supplying rural areas; over 70 per cent of Oman's water is distributed this way, and 55 per cent of crops depend on a *falaj*.

Construction takes ingenuity and experience as well as back-breaking effort. The water must flow down a gentle, steady gradient, so channels can be found carved high up on the steep sides of wadis, passing over aqueducts or through tunnels and even siphons. Friction and leakage are reduced by plastering them with a smooth waterproof cement. Some systems, centuries old, divide the supply from one source into more than 300 channels.

The tapping of underground supplies is especially complicated and dangerous. Their discovery used to depend on water diviners, who could detect a source as deep as 50 m (over 160 ft). A tunnel is excavated by digging vertical shafts every 25 m (80 ft) or so and linking them up. On the surface, spoil heaps at the top of each shaft show the line taken. The small wiry men of the Awama tribe are expert at this work; heat and lack of air restricts them to 20 minutes at a time in the narrowest passages.

Similarities to the ancient *qanat* system, still seen in Iran today, once led scholars to credit the Persians with introducing it to Oman around the 6th century BC, but it now appears to have been developed here in the Arabian peninsula even earlier.

Surface channels are usually roofed over as far as the edge of a village, to prevent pollution (and to ensure that bans on watering animals and washing are observed). Ownership of the *falaj* is divided into many shares, determined by the rate of flow and the time—traditionally read from a sundial, nowadays a clock, at the distribution point. The first water is drawn off for drinking and cooking; below that point there are washing areas for men and women. Washing of clothes and cooking pots comes next, and finally the water enters the irrigation channels of the share-owner's garden.

Nizwa's golden fort is still impressive.

if you have the time—overnight stays. Not only picturesque; it is also the centre of the Omani craft industry. On Friday mornings, people pour in from all over the region to buy and sell livestock and produce at the open-air market. At other times, you'll probably see merchants selling wares from the backs of lorries in front of the blue-domed mosque. But go behind the mosque to find the covered **souk**, largely rebuilt in recent years but still fascinating. If you venture into the back streets you're likely to come across khanjar-makers at work.

The 17th-century **fort**, on the other side of the mosque, served for 300 years as palace, prison and seat of government. Its 87 great, round, golden tower, the biggest in Oman, was built in the reign of Sultan bin Saif. It was designed for the new era of the cannon, with gunports commanding a 360-degree field of fire. As recently as the 1950s, it was the headquarters of the imam, at that time in revolt against the sultan.

Bahla

An oasis and huge fortress enclosed by a mud-brick wall 12 km (7 miles) long, and reputed as the dwelling place of magicians, witches and soothsayers, this neighbour of Nizwa was the capital city in the 15th century. Oman's diligent restoration teams face a daunting task here; the sprawling, dilapidated ruins, designated a World Heritage Site by UNESCO, tower over 50 m (165 ft) above the surrounding plain. They dwarf today's town, known for its potters who turn out jars and kitchen ware, fired in traditional clay ovens—you are welcome to visit their workshops. The central square of the small modern town is a lively market, part of it highly specialized, for Bahla is a centre of the date trade.

The **fort** at Jabrin, standing in the middle of the plain near Bahla and 50 km (31 miles) west of Nizwa, was built in the

Dealing in Dates

The centre of Bahla at market time is crowded and the atmosphere reminiscent of the trading floor of a commodity exchange in one of the world's financial capitals. Dealers shout and gesticulate, bargains are struck, promises of future delivery made with a minimum of paperwork. The difference, apart from the open-air setting under a blazing sun, is in the commodity, for here it is dates. Sacks of them lie about, from which samples are constantly being taken and sniffed, squeezed and tasted. Hopeful merchants hold out handfuls for the buyers to try. Clearly there is a lot of expertise involved: anyone who thinks a date is just a date should pay a visit to Bahla.

second half of the 17th century as a fortress-palace. One of the finest examples of traditional Omani architecture, it still guards the tomb of its builder, Bilarab bin Sultan, who died in 1692. Inside, the flowing designs of its painted ceilings, such as the one in the hall of the Sun and Moon, echo the patterns of Persian carpets. The intricately carved wooden balconies and plaster grilles add to the air of elegance.

Jabrin was extensively restored in the 1980s and fur-

Dates by the barrowful in the streets of Bahla.

nished with various household items to illustrate the traditional life of the region. In case of a siege, its cisterns held plenty of water, and its deep cellars could store a year's supply of dates—practically a complete food, according to the guardians. "Dates and water, that's all they needed to live on!"

Tanuf, reached from the road between Bahla and Nizwa, was the scene of tribal warfare in the 1950s. All is quiet these days; you'll find an attractive village and an elaborate *falaj* system.

Also set in a wadi in the mountains north of Bahla, the village of **Al-Hamra** with its clay houses is worth a diversion.

You can hardly distinguish the village of **Misfa** from the cliff face from which it is hewn. Shaded by lemon trees, little streets wind upwards to the different levels of houses, like caves carved out of the rock, with spiral staircases leading to dizzying terraces. Children's faces peer inquisitively from upper windows, only to vanish when you look up at them.

89

Sohar

On the coast north of Muscat, Sohar has come down in the world. Once the biggest town on the coast, it now occupies only a fraction of the area it covered a thousand years ago. The legendary home of Sindbad the Sailor, hero of Arab folk tales, it was, according to the 10th-century geographer al-Istakhri, "the greatest seaport of Islam and the most populous and wealthy town in Oman". The Portuguese took it early in the 16th century and made it one of their strongholds guarding the sea routes to India. Above the town rise the six towers of its fort, dazzling white against the blue sea and sky.

Prehistoric remains show that copper was mined in the area in ancient times, perhaps as early as 3000 BC. Narrow tunnels have been found, bored through the rock to the richest deposits of ore, and old spoil heaps and slag from smelting operations dot the hillsides. Mining seems to have stopped around AD 900: it has recently been resumed after a gap of over a thousand years.

Buraimi Oasis

Inland, across the mountains from Sohar, the large, well-watered Buraimi Oasis is divided between Oman and the United Arab Emirates. You can travel to it by road, but you need

---

Back to the Wild

The Arabian oryx, a handsome antelope with long, back-swept horns, a snow-white coat and black facial markings, is the largest of the region's wild animals. Able to survive the harshest conditions, it once roamed over most of Arabia, able to outpace its only enemy, man. Then came the all-terrain vehicle and the automatic rifle. The oryx was hunted to near extinction: the last were shot in central Oman in the 1970s.

Fortunately, for once, conservationists were a step ahead of the hunters. A few captured animals and a handful donated by zoos became the nucleus of a herd kept in parks in the US. They soon multiplied, and it became possible to bring about 20 back to Oman. Living at first in pens, they bred well, and several dozen were released into the desert, to be watched over by Bedouin of the Harasi tribe. The process has not been easy. Many have succumbed to disease or, unable to adapt from a sheltered captive life, starved. But hopes remain high that in the long run the graceful oryx will again be safely established as a living symbol of its homeland.

a permit from the Immigration Department of the Ministry of the Interior. Once there, you can cross freely between the Omani side and the sprawling modern city of Al Ain in the UAE.

Until the 1950s, the border in this area was ill-defined. An attempt by Saudi Arabia to seize the oasis was thwarted by Sheikh Zayed (later the ruler of Abu Dhabi and UAE President) and the British-officered Trucial Oman Scouts.

Buraimi was a key trading post and crossroads of caravan routes for over a thousand years, and its souks and livestock markets remain a magnet for the Bedouin of the region. Several of the picturesque old forts built to defend it still stand, in contrast to air-conditioned offices and luxury hotels. The battlements of the restored 18th-century **Al-Khandaq fort** make a great vantage point for looking out over the oasis and the desert beyond.

Musandam

Cut off from the rest of Oman by UAE territory, a mountainous peninsula and a handful of islands form the southern side of the Strait of Hormuz, facing the Iranian shore only about 50 km (30 miles) away. A procession of super tankers passes into the Arabian (or Persian) Gulf, and out again, carrying a significant share of the world's oil. They stick to the Oman side of the strait, watched over by the sultan's navy.

South of Muscat

The road swings inland and then back to the sea at the old town of **Qurayat**, with its fort, of course, and endless sandy beach. Four-wheel-drive vehicles can take you on excursions along rocky tracks through the Eastern Hajar mountains and down into wadis lush and green with palm groves and orchards.

To reach Sur, further along the coast, the main road from Muscat makes a long loop south of the Eastern Hajar, skirting the **Wahiba Sands**, a great tract of sharp-edged *barkhan* dunes. Despite initial appearances, this is no lifeless desert; the fragile environment supports a remarkable range of plant and animal life, and has been the subject of a detailed study by scientists. The Bedouin tribes who live on the edge of the sands graze hundreds of their camels and thousands of goats on fresh green growth that springs up if it has recently rained, and on unpalatable-looking thorny scrub if it hasn't.

If you are lucky, you may spot a rare, shy gazelle picking its way daintily among the 91

A dying art—drilling holes by bow and string.

dunes, or hardly seeming to touch the ground as it bounds for the horizon.

Sur

With its natural harbour and perfect location, Sur was a major port for centuries: Marco Polo called in during his voyage in the 13th century and reported that it was much frequented by merchant ships from India, bringing in spices and other goods and carrying away fine war horses.

It's hardly so busy today, but the beaches are wonderful. **Snisla Fort** with its decorated "wedding-cake" tower has been restored. At the **dhow-builders'**

yard just out of town, you'll see traditional wooden craft under construction, using methods that have scarcely changed in centuries. Drills are still driven by a bow and string, and the shipwrights search in their stocks of timber for natural joints, which are stronger than man-made. One concession to modernity: the dhows are fitted with motors and most of them have been stripped of their sails. Nearby, a free ferry crosses the creek to **Ayga**, a small village where the dhow-builders live. It too has a superb fort.

Leaving the harbour loaded with ice, Sur's fishing dhows spend up to two weeks at sea before returning with the catch. Part of it is dried and used for feeding cattle.

You can take short excursion by dhow to **Ras al-Hadd**, the headland east of Sur known for the turtles which swim offshore and make their way up the beach to lay their eggs.

Next to the sea northwest of Sur, the ruins of **Qalhat** support Marco Polo's account of its wealth and magnificence. Although it fell into a decline in late medieval times and was afterwards abandoned, you can still see the outline of its streets, part of the city walls and the impressive brick tower of the Bibi Maryam tomb.

Dhofar

Some 1,000 km (620 miles) to the southwest of Muscat on the Arabian Sea, palm-shaded **Salalah** is the provincial capital of Dhofar and the second city of Oman. Regular flights link the two centres, as well as comfortable long-distance buses making the 13-hour journey on the smooth, well-engineered highway.

Once a significant port trading in the frankincense extracted from the trees that have grown for centuries on the neighbouring hills, Salalah is now a modern town which has managed to keep much of its charm and character. Small white bougainvillaea-covered houses rub shoulders with office towers; souks and department stores teem with visitors, and the newest and oldest mosques stand side by side. The coast offers superb beaches sheltered by cliffs, with pure white sand lapped by clear, warm seas and soft winds whispering in the nearby coconut and banana plantations. Thanks to the summer monsoon, it is relatively cool and green all through the summer when the rest of the country is baking.

The **museum**, in the Cultural Centre on Ar-Robat Road, contains stones inscribed in ancient 93

Frankincense

If you want to take someone a kingly gift, buy some frankincense. In ancient times it was considered to be one of the highest tributes one could offer, as the Magi did to the infant Jesus. Frankincense was thought to have medicinal properties, and was used in embalming—pieces were found in the tomb of Tutankhamun—but most was burned in religious rites; it was believed that prayers were carried to heaven by its scented fumes.

There are only three places in the world where the tall bushes of *Boswellia carterii* or *Boswellia sacra* that produce it will grow: Yemen, northern Somalia and the Dhofar region of southern Oman. The aromatic gum flows from incisions cut in the tree trunks; it hardens into dark amber- or golden-coloured lumps which burn easily thanks to their high oil content.

During the Roman era, it is said that over 3,000 tonnes of it were exported annually from Arabia, carried north by ship and camel caravan for distribution to the cities of the Empire. When Rome declined, Christians and Muslims continued to use incense in their ceremonies, but in far smaller quantities. Exports fell to a few tonnes per year and finally, a modern synthetic substitute developed in Rome destroyed the trade altogether. But local women still scent their hair by wafting it in the smoke, and this gave a modern *parfumier* the idea of creating a new fragrance based on frankincense as well as many floral extracts. You'll find it on sale in Oman, and around the world, in bottles shaped like the handle of a *khanjar* dagger.

South Arabian script, and displays of pottery, tools and weapons, traditional costumes and jewellery. Some of the objects on show have been excavated from the **Al-Balid** quarter of Salalah, dating from the 11th century. Excavations there have revealed the remains of a once-magnificent 13th-century mosque, whose roof of carved beams was supported by 136 columns.

The New Souk is nothing special, just a food market, but you may like to visit the **Gold Souk**, on Al-Nahdah Street, to see the selection of oriental and modern gold and silver jewellery.

Along the coast, **Khor Rori**, 40 km (25 miles) east of Salalah, was once the ancient trading port of Sumhuram. This was where the precious frankincense was loaded on ships for export to the east, or on seagoing rafts which took it to Qana in Yemen and thence to Damascus, Egypt and Jerusalem. According to tradition, King Solomon himself sailed into the harbour, long since silted up. Ruins, dating mainly from the 1st century AD, are now a rather nondescript archaeological site.

In the nearby coastal village of **Taqa**, traditional rafts and boats are still made and used as in ancient times. The house of the *wali* (local chief) is strikingly fortified. Quarries at Taqa provide much of the stone used to face Salalah's handsomer buildings. About 20 km (12 miles) away at **Mirbat**, many of the houses are built in traditional Omani style, with elaborate carved doors; there's also the inevitable fort.

Mughsail, 30 km (18 miles) west of Salalah, has long, beautiful beaches, sheltered by rocky headlands pierced by caves and blowholes through which the sea spouts in rough weather.

Inland

The Qara mountains *(Jebel al Qara)* are the home of the mountain tribes, with their large

A camel ambles past sardines left to dry in the sun.

A watchtower looms over palms shading an oasis.

herds of camels and cattle. Here and there a cluster of palm trees betrays the presence of a little village; on rocky outcrops ruined watchtowers point like arthritic fingers to the sky. Families cultivate their land with an ox-drawn plough; the stone channels of an ancient *falaj* bring water from a central well to irrigate fields of onions and garlic, date palms and orchards of cherry and citrus trees.

Excursions into the Jebel al-Qara and its wadis by four-wheel drive vehicle include the natural springs of **Ain Arzat**, the well-watered Wadi Darbat, and the pools of **Ayun**. It's worth a diversion to see the mysterious prehistoric standing stones in **Wadi Ghudun**. Generally grouped in threes, they may mark ancient burial sites. **Wadi Hanun** was once a collecting point for the frankincense where it was stored before being carried north by camel caravan or south to the ancient port of Sumhuram.

The area around **Thumrait**, 80 km (50 miles) inland, is noted for its wonderful desert scenery. To the north stretches the long black line of the asphalt highway to Muscat, following an ancient caravan route through the Jiddah. Harsh as this landscape may seem, it is home to the Harasi, a Bedouin tribe that probably originated in Ethiopia and speak their own language. Old watering holes are marked by a few crumbling buildings sinking slowly into oblivion, replaced by their modern equivalent—rest houses and petrol stations.

Still further inland, straddling the border with Saudi Arabia, is the fabled **Rub al-Khali** ("The Empty Quarter") a moonscape of sand dunes, sparse thorn bushes and rocks where only the hardiest Bedouin or the best-prepared expeditions can travel.

Eating Out

Many visitors choose to dine in hotels where the menus are international but with the bonus of fresh locally caught fish and seafood—the prawns and spiny lobsters can be excellent. An Indian curry or two and some Arabic specialities add a touch of exotica. Alcoholic drinks are available in the larger and more expensive hotels: elsewhere the choice is restricted to water and soft drinks, sometimes fruit juice.

The big towns have good Chinese and Lebanese restaurants, sometimes in upmarket versions. To eat economically, head for an Indian restaurant, where the food will be tasty if not always varied. The Muscat area has the same fast-food outlets as any other capital city, most of these establishments being centred in Ruwi.

Should you be invited to an Omani home (which is not unlikely as the people are very hospitable, especially in small settlements), you will be expected to remove your shoes and sit on a rug or mat on the floor. Take care that when you sit the soles of your feet do not point towards anyone: it would be considered an insulting gesture in most Arab countries. And remember to eat, drink and offer things using only the right hand.

Tea or coffee is usually offered, and you would be very 97

Refreshment is at hand beneath the palm trees.

discourteous to refuse it. The coffee is excellent and often spiced with cardamom, which gives it a greenish tinge. If you don't want any more, cover the cup with your right hand. It's polite to accept a second cup, but you should not drink more than three.

All the outside influences mean that genuinely local dishes are few, They are based mainly on lamb, sometimes elaborately prepared, subtly spiced and almost always accompanied with rice. A whole roast lamb is the centrepiece of most feasts; on lesser occasions there are kebabs; chunks of lamb or meatballs grilled on a skewer. For dessert there may be *halwa*, made from nuts, honey, butter and spices, or fruit, and dates—to an Omani, especially someone from the interior, no meal is complete without them.

Shopping

Silver jewellery is probably the best buy in Oman. Traditional designs are intricately worked, and range from delightful little kohl boxes to ornamental chest pieces, sometimes with bronze, gold, coloured glass or old coins worked in. You are not likely to find anything more than 50 years old, as traditionally most jewellery was part of a bride's dowry, and was melted down after its owner's death.

Jewellers also sell the handsome silver Maria Theresia dollar *(thaler)* coins, first minted in late 18th-century Imperial Austria. Despite the date 1780 which appears on them, most were produced much later, from the 19th century right up to modern times—silversmiths from Beirut to Dubai are still making perfect copies, with the right silver content of about 20 grams.

A symbol of virility, the beautiful curved *khanjar* daggers, with finely worked sheaths, scabbards and belts, were made traditionally with handles of rhinoceros horn. Though shopkeepers may try to convince you they are selling you the real thing, the handles nowadays are generally made from plastic or wood. In any case it is forbidden to import rhino horn into most countries, the rhinoceros being an endangered species.

Brass and copper objects make attractive souvenirs, particularly the coffee pots with their curved spouts. You'll also find enticing selections of fabric from many exotic places, especially Kashmir shawls (which many Omani men wear as turbans), highly coloured dress lengths, saris, robes and caftans.

There's a whole range of spices to bring Middle Eastern and Indian flavours to your cooking, and fragrant rose or orange blossom water from the terraced gardens of the Green Mountain.

Weights and Measures

Today's traders operate in a system as comprehensible as anywhere in the world, and in a straightforward currency, the stable Omani rial. But three decades ago, the complexities were notorious. Many kinds of money circulated: those of all Oman's neighbours as well as pounds sterling, Indian rupees, US dollars and especially the celebrated Maria Theresia thaler. The values and weights of various multiples and fractions of these relics (5, 6, 12, 20, 24, 120) made up competing but overlapping regional systems. Few outsiders and not all locals ever understood them, so there was general relief when simplification was decreed as one of the earliest moves towards modernization. One exception survives: silver is weighed in tolas (the word deriving from thaler). One tola = 11.75g.

99

Practical Information

Currency. The Omani Rial (OR or OMR), divided into 1,000 *baisa*. Coins from 5 to 500 baisa; notes from 100 baisa to 50 rials.

Climate. Generally hot and humid on the coast, cooler in the mountains. Around Muscat, the small amount of rain falls mainly between December and March. In the south, the rainy season is from June to September.

Clothing. Lightweight washable cottons are recommended, with something warmer for nights in the desert. Dress modestly, to comply with Muslim traditions. Shorts are frowned upon, whether for men or women. Trousers are acceptable for women, as long as they are loosely cut: avoid anything tight or revealing. Sunglasses and a sun hat are essential.

Electricity. 220/240V AC, 50 Hz.

Health. Precautions against malaria are advisable, although the risk is small.

Hours. Banks open Sat to Wed 8 a.m. to noon, Thurs 8–11 a.m. Offices open Sat to Wed 8 a.m.–1 p.m. and 4–7 p.m., Thurs 8 a.m. to 1 p.m. Shops open 8 a.m. to 1 p.m. and 4 p.m. to 8 p.m. Sat to Thurs. Some shops in Mutrah souk open on Friday evening too.

Language. Arabic. English is generally understood in the Muscat area and in business and government circles.

Photography. Ask permission first. Men and children are usually quite happy to be photographed; women will usually refuse, or turn away as soon as they see a camera. You should not take photos of any military sites.

Telephone. The system is modern and efficient. The outgoing international code is 00.

Time. GMT + 4.

Tipping. Where a service charge has not been added, 10–15% should be added to restaurant bills. Taxi drivers and porters also expect a tip.

Water. Tap water is drinkable in the cities and towns. In the villages, stick to bottled drinks.

Photos: pp. 69, 74, 77, 89, 95, 96, 98 Bernard Joliat; p. 79 Pankaj Shah; pp. 81, 84, 87, 92 Martin Gostelow

YEMEN

Queen of Sheba Land

Yemen lies in that part of the Arabian peninsula the Romans called *Arabia Felix*—"Happy Arabia"—as a tribute to its arable land and the prosperity it enjoyed from exporting frankincense and myrrh to the Ancient World. Balkis, Queen of Sheba (Saba), ruled the Sabaean people about 1,000 BC, and the Book of Kings in the Old Testament tells of the rich gifts she brought to the court of Solomon. Alexander the Great was so taken with Yemen that he wanted to make it his home after he returned from India, but death nipped his dream in the bud.

For most of its history, the country was a collection of kingdoms or sultanates, sometimes warring. From these disparate factions, two modern states emerged in the 1960s: the former Yemen Arab Republic, or North Yemen, and the ex-People's Democratic Republic, or South Yemen. In 1990 they proclaimed their unification, calling the new state the "Yemen Republic". With Sanaa as its capital, it has a population of 11 million people for about 530,000 sq km (205,000 sq miles).

The Yemeni people are almost 100 per cent Muslim—both Sunni and Shia. Infant mortality is high, educational standards are low and women have traditionally been ascribed an inferior place in society. The south is trying to rectify this situation and has succeeded to the extent that in Aden, at any rate, girls and boys attend primary school and increasingly women go unveiled. Health standards are being improved.

The southern part of the country, corresponding to the area which Britain controlled from 1839 to 1967, had almost no industry when it attained independence, except in the Port of Aden commanding the entrance to the Suez Canal. It was badly affected by the closure of the canal after the Egypt-Israeli war but has regained its importance for international shipping.

Yemen, a country with few natural resources, is attempting to modernize its economy. As well as its traditional activities (fishing, agriculture), it has been quite a significant producer of oil since 1985. The country's most important source of foreign exchange, however, came, until recently, from the earnings of the many Yemeni men working abroad.

Behind the face of a developing nation is a world of fiercely guarded tradition. Yemeni men often wear a kilt *(futa)* or a wide-sleeved robe *(zana)*. They cover their heads with a stiff skull-cap used as a basis on which to drape their turban, a masterpiece of uninhibited self-expression, often set off by a bunch of flowers. The dagger *(jambiyya)* is both an arm and a symbol of pride.

Women in Aden may be seen either in European clothes or wearing the shapeless black *shaider*. In the countryside, their dress is colourful and may take the form of trousers caught in at the ankles and an embroidered tunic. Veils are still regularly worn. Country women, especially in the Hadhramawt area, sometimes have on a straw hat with a high, pointed crown, like a witch's hat in fairy tales.

All told, Yemen is an exciting blend of modern ports and inland towns and villages continuing in their age-old ways.

A Brief History

1,000 BC– 2nd century BC	Kingdom of Sheba. The country supplies the ancient world with frankincense and myrrh, transported by sea and overland by caravan. In 115 BC the Himyarite dynasty is in control with its capital at present-day Dhafar.
4th–7th centuries AD	Judaism and Christianity are introduced. Conflicts erupt between the two religions, and in 525 the Christian Ethiopians intervene. Their presence is short-lived and is followed by Persian domination until 628 when the governor is converted to the new religion of Islam. Christianity fades shortly after the introduction of Islam but a Jewish colony lives on in Yemen until the creation of Israel in 1948.
16th century	The Turks arrive in 1517 and remain for a century.
19th century	The British take Aden in 1839; it is of prime importance for their access to India. They administer the south from Bombay. The opening of the Suez Canal in 1869 makes Aden even more vital. In 1872 the Turks once more occupy large parts of Yemen.
20th century	After World War I, an imamate, the Kingdom of Yemen, is established in the north. Aden officially becomes a British Crown Colony in 1937. In 1958 the Kingdom of

Yemen joins the short-lived United Arab States with Egypt and Syria. The 1960s mark the outbreak of revolution and civil war—in 1962 the north forms the Yemen Arab Republic, or North Yemen; Aden and the south achieve independence in 1967, and in 1970 declare the People's Democratic Republic, a Marxist state. The two Yemens bury the hachet to form a united Yemen Republic in May 1990; the fledgling country's fortunes drop dramatically when Saudi Arabia expels 800,000 Yemeni workers during the 1990–91 Gulf War. The world nods approval over Yemen's first multi-party elections in 1993, but the precariousness of the union is revealed in May 1994 when the south attempts briefly to break away but fails.

Around Happy Arabia

The topography of Yemen varies from tropical coastal fishing villages to temperate high plateaus fecund with cereals and fruits. The scene is endlessly enchanting, whether you are visiting nomadic tribal lands of the north or a modern urban agglomeration with a maze of an old city at its heart.

Aden

Arriving by sea your first sight is the impressive backdrop of dark volcanic mountains, with Aden nestling at their foot. The largest of these is Mount Shamsan, which rises to a height of 540 m (1,775 ft).

The city itself is divided into several districts, Steamer Point (now called Tawahi) being the passenger port. You may like to look in at the famous **Crescent Hotel**; its elegance fled with the British but you can still sense a certain ghostly colonial grandeur. The country's history comes to life at the **National Museum**, one of the most important in the country. Its treasures include a group of half-lifesize alabaster statues unearthed from the excavations of various towns of the Awsan kingdom, a rival of Saba.

Maala is a dock and industrial area, through which you have to pass to reach **Crater**, a district dramatically bound in on three sides by barren rock. There are still a few old houses worth seeing among the modern office and apartment blocks.

Make a point of visiting the extraordinary **Tawila Cisterns** on Mount Shamsan: 18 of them, thought to have been built

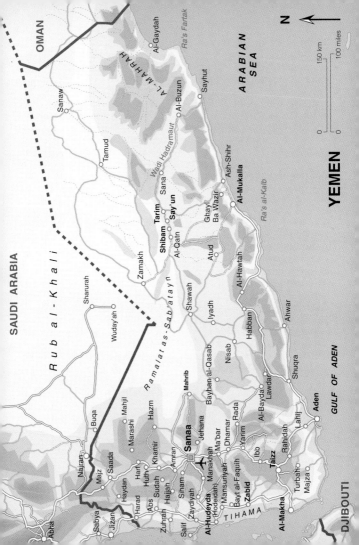

by the Himyarites in the 1st century AD. The idea was to catch the water gushing down from the mountaintop. You can still see remains of the special marble paste used to line the tanks. In the surrounding garden stands the **Ethnographical Museum**, where you can admire textiles and daggers.

Find time also to visit the **Aidrus Mosque** and an edifice known simply as the "Minaret", thought to be the remains of an 8th-century mosque. The dazzling white tower was restored in the 18th century.

Among the many forts and old walls, the most interesting is on Mount Seera Island, a spot that has become a seaside resort for local people. **Gold Mohur Beach** is marked by a lighthouse at the southern end and a hill fortified with ancient Turkish cannons; Alghadir Beach has a central hill with remains of old fortifications.

Taiz

One of the roads leading to the north from Aden passes through Taiz, a former capital of Yemen. Its location at 1,400 m (4,600 ft) in the foot-hills of Jabal Sabir, the highest mountain in Taiz Province, assures it more moderate temperatures than the coastal towns. One highlight is the lively **market** at the north-ern wall of the old city, in which unveiled women merchants, noted for their tough bargaining, are to be seen—a rare sight in Yemen on both accounts.

The city is dominated by the **Fortress of Cairo** high on its cliff, out of bounds for tourists as it is in military use. They can, however, enter the former palace of Imam Ahmad, now the **National Museum**. Everything has been left just as it was when the imam died in 1962, supposedly to demonstrate the social iniquity of his rule prior to the revolution in the north. **Salah Palace** also belonged to the imam and is similarly a museum.

Sanaa

Once you have seen Sanaa (2,350 m or 7,750 ft altitude), the "pearl of Arabia" and Yemen's capital, you will understand why UNESCO saw fit in 1984 to take the magical city under its protection. The ensemble of mud-brick ochre "skyscrapers", ornamented in elaborate white alabaster and plasterwork and multi-coloured windowpanes, is one of the most beautiful sights in the world.

Yemeni folklore relates that Sanaa was founded by Noah's son Shem. Hence the town answers to the nickname "Sam City". The story is also told that

Green terraces at At-Tawila northwest of Sanaa offer proof that Yemen is not all sand-coloured.

during the period of the Sabaean and Himyarite kingdoms in Yemen, Sanaa had a great palace 20 storeys high, as well as a splendid cathedral that drew Christian pilgrims from all over Arabia. Nothing remains of either of these edifices, but the memories are kept alive.

With the advent of Islam, Sanaa's fortunes alternated between prosperity, when it was the capital either of a region or of all of Yemen, and destruction, as sultans seized power from each other. The last conquerors were the Turks, who held the city for a second time from 1872 to 1912. The civil war in the north in the 1960s began in Sanaa. After it ended, the city began to expand outside its walls and the population exploded as well. Today it is a 107 bustling city of 430,000 complete with traffic jams.

Within the modern exterior, Sanaa has one of the largest completely preserved walled cities, or **medina**, in the Arab world. Its eastern part, at the very least, begs to be explored. Here are found the most imposing of the fabulous tower houses. Don't stint on film supplies, as photogenic subjects present themselves everywhere as you wander among the beautiful houses, mosques and souks. Note, too, the many *hammams*, or bathhouses, dating from the Turkish era. You may be lucky enough to catch a glimpse of some of the private gardens adjoining the houses and mosques, pleasant oases in the urban maze. The western part of the medina is less exotic,

Wadi Dhahr near Sanaa harbours the Rock Palace, an imam's summer residence perched on a rock.

as it consists largely of newer buildings. But even there a few beautiful old houses remain, as well as the old embassies and the former Jewish quarter.

Bab al-Yaman, or Gate of Yemen, is the break in the old city wall at the southwest part of the medina. The square here is animated at most any time of day. The largest city market in Yemen, **Suq al-Milh**, begins at the gate and extends half a kilometre north within the medina. It is grouped into some 40 areas, each specializing in a particular kind of merchandise. Outside of the medina, to the east, lies the **Suq al-Qat**, a market devoted primarily to the green leaf beloved of Yemeni men (see box).

The Suq al-Milh snakes its way past the **Great Mosque**, built around AD 630, when the Prophet Mohammed was still alive. It is certainly worth inquiring whether you may enter to see its richly decorated interior. Some of Sanaa's other **mosques** can be appreciated from the exterior, such as the al-'Aqil Mosque, whose beautiful minaret rises over Suq al-Milh. You can also step back to get a good view of Qubbat al-Bakiliya, on al-Liqiya Street in the easternmost sector of the medina. It dates from the early 1600s, when the Turks first occupied Yemen. Not surprisingly, its numerous cupolas reflect the Turkish style.

The **National Museum** will give you a good overview of

What's Qat?

The former People's Democratic Republic did its best to quash the qat-chewing habit, but it's still enjoyed throughout Yemen. *Qat* (pronounced gat) is a green leaf with mild euphoriant qualities which grows in the high country. It is customary for almost every Yemeni man to spend the greater part of the afternoon in a social group chewing his way through about four bunches of qat shoots, bought fresh each day. The leaves are not swallowed but held in a wad in the side of the cheek and spat out at the end of the session. Cigarette and hookah-smoking are part of the ritual and the chewers refresh themselves frequently with sips of water, lightly flavoured with cinnamon or clove—although cola-based drinks are catching on. Women chew less than men: they say it spoils the shape of the face.

It is maintained that the leaf is not addictive. It can have harmful physical effects, but the real damage is economic. All activity stops for the daily ritual, large sums are spent, families suffer and coffee plantations are torn up and replaced by this more remunerative crop.

109

Yemen's history, covering pre-Islamic ancient kingdoms such as that of Saba, and Islamic times. The museum's third floor highlights folk culture.

Marib

Marib is the old capital of the kingdom of Saba. Lying east of Sanaa on the ancient frankincense trade route, it prospered from the taxes levied on passing caravans. The Great Dam Marib constructed in the 8th century BC to irrigate fields of cereals and palm oases was a stunning feat of engineering in its day. It was washed away in AD 570. Head for the **archaeological sites** to see the remains of Sabaean temples and the ruins of the sluice gates of the ancient dam. The old village on a hill apart from the new town is made up of mud skyscrapers, mostly abandoned. Integrated into the foundations of the houses are stones from ancient monuments, bearing inscriptions and designs.

Hodeidah

The city of Hodeidah is the hub of the region known as Tihama, the coastlands of the Red Sea. These hot, sand-blown flatlands with their predominantly black peoples make a contrast to the cooler highlands with their Semitic population.

Slavery and long-term migration from East Africa account for the Tihama's racially diverse makeup. As the source of almost half of the country's agricultural production, the Tihama is Yemen's most economically important region.

Hodeidah is a relatively young city. It was only from 1830 onwards that the Turks began to turn it into an efficient port in response to the British development of Aden. Progress was set back when the city was bombarded during World War I. In 1934 the Tihama was coveted by Saudi Arabia, but since the skirmishes of that year between the two countries, Hodeidah has been able to develop in tranquillity. At the time of reunification of the two Yemens it ranked as Yemen's second most important port.

A stroll through the city's oldest part near the market area can be rewarding. The typical old Red Sea houses here are three or four storeys high and feature wooden balconies or window covers—Turkish style—and interesting plaster-ornamented walls. You might be surprised to find Indian decorations on some of the doorways—executed by the craftsmen who used to follow in the wake of sailors and traders to the ports of the Red Sea coast.

Truth be told, there are few other charms to Hodeidah. Its touristic importance lies more in its convenience as a stopping point en route to more interesting outlying sights. About an hour away to the south by road, for example, **Bayt al-Faqih** attracts visitors from far and wide to its famous Friday market, established in the early 1700s for trading in coffee beans. (The word "mocha" derives from the nearby port of Al-Makha, or Mokka, where rich coffee merchants exported their products in the 17th century.) Apart from coffee, you can buy every sort of fruit and vegetable and handicraft.

Zabid

Zabid ranks as one of Yemen's oldest towns. The university

Shibam in Wadi Hadhramawt shows what a little imagination can do with mud bricks.

here dates from the 9th century; its biggest claim to fame is the creation of algebra by one of its scholars. Though much diminished now, from the 13th to the 15th centuries it was the focal point of Sunni teaching for the southern part of the Islamic world, and the town harboured 236 mosques. The points of interest today are its old walled souk, some large houses—sober on the street side, but splendidly ornamented within—and the citadel's palace, now a government building.

Mukalla

Capital of Yemen's largest province, in the eastern part of the country, Mukalla is a wealthy seaport and fishing centre on the Gulf of Aden. Its white waterfront houses, with their engraved wooden window blinds and balconies and turquoise decorations, make a pretty sight. When you walk around the old town, note the handsome **Rawdha Mosque**, one of the most notable of Mukalla's many beautiful places of worship.

The **Al-Mukalla Museum**, near the bay, is housed in what was once the palace of the sultans. The building has been renovated to display folklore and antiquities of the region.

Visitors to Mukalla shouldn't fail to venture north into the **Wadi Hadhramawt**, one of Yemen's major attractions. The biggest river valley in the Arabian Peninsula, the wadi runs for 160 km (95 miles), fertile and green on its banks, through stone-strewn desert plateaus. It is located on the ancient incense route—frankincense was in fact grown on its banks—and was prosperous in those bygone centuries, when its waters were used in intricate irrigation systems.

It was here in the wadi that Yemen's tower-house style of building originated. In the dry season, mudbrick-making can

Sartorial Splendour

What does the well-dressed Yemeni male wear? In the West, a gentleman puts on a tie to appear at his best; here at the edge of the Arabian Peninsula he slings a Kalashnikov over his shoulder. The dagger worn at the waist has been a requisite Yemeni macho ornament for eons, but nowadays the average man has a wide choice of weaponry: souks are stocked with old hunting guns, automatic rifles, bazookas and hand grenades. Not to worry: it's mostly show—all that steel is reserved for harmlessly shooting off a few rounds with a flourish on special occasions like weddings or Friday outings, and, of course, for legitimate self-defence.

be see everywhere. At **Shibam** you encounter the tower houses of mud bricks at their most exquisite: the southern counterpoint to Sanaa. Here are assembled some 500 beautiful "skyscrapers" of as many as 13 storeys, giving rise to the epithet "Manhattan of the desert". As it did for Sanaa, UNESCO has undertaken a programme of preservation. The best thing to do here is to wander around the town's narrow streets along with the goats, and to photograph the town at sunset from the cliffs above the suburb of Sihayl.

Further into the wadi lies **Say'un**, largest town in the valley. For 500 years, until the 1967 revolution, a North Yemeni tribe made it their capital, building some of the most beautiful mosques in all of Yemen. Dominating the "town of a million palm trees" is the stunning white-plastered Sultan's Palace. The archaeological and folklore museum installed within fills only a small part of the immense structure. The Tomb of Habshi also cries out for attention with its turquoise splendor, but it dates only from the 1910s.

Tarim has been an important centre of Islamic teaching for centuries, and it boasts some 365 mosques. The 50-m-high

Proud Yemeni and prize possesions: rifle and ceremonial dagger.

square minaret of the most famous, Al-Muhdar, is depicted on virtually every brochure describing the wadi. The town is distinctive for its displaced architecture—South-East Asian baroque! It seems that many of the Yemenis returning home from places like Java and Singapore—numbering 300,000 in the 1930s—were rich enough to build huge palaces.

113

Eating Out

Traditional Yemeni cooking is done in a *tannur* or pottery oven set in sun-baked bricks. Cereals are the basic foodstuff, served with vegetables, or meat. In the south a lot of fish and rice is eaten.

Normally a meal begins with radishes and onions, followed by sweet dishes flavoured with honey and butter. Then come savoury dishes using mutton or beef if they are available. The national speciality is *helba*, a kind of thin stew which is eaten using flat *khobz* bread as a spoon.

While knives and forks are used as well, the traditional way for a family to eat is with the right hand from a communal bowl. In larger gatherings there are separate receptacles for men and women.

Tea may be served but the favourite drink is *qishr*, coffee made from the husks and flavoured with ginger, cinnamon or cloves. It was first choice in the harems of Turkey and is often known as "sultan's coffee". It is poured into small, handleless cups (you hold them from underneath on the tips of your fingers) and is the usual beverage offered visitors.

Tourist hotels serve European food.

Shopping

The silver markets in the souks of Sanaa, Taiz and Hodeidah are a popular hunting ground for tourists, but be aware that the objects may contain relatively little silver and be treated to look old. Notwithstanding, there are some pretty necklaces, earrings, bangles and chains to be found, the silver often combined with coral, pearls, amber, glass or ceramic. Gold jewellery may be of good value, as supposedly it is sold strictly by the gram, with no value added for the craftsmanship. *Do* have an idea of gold prices in advance so that you can be sure to get fair value.

The curved tribesman's dagger worn by men on a belt, known as the *jambiyya*, makes a good purchase. The model worn by the elite classes, the *dhuma*, is richly ornamented with silver and gold. A water pipe *(madaa)* will require plenty of space to carry home, as it typically stands a metre (3 ft) high, and a bulky tripod stand goes along with it.

The quality of the sound of cassette recordings will vary enormously, but they are inexpensive. Others ideas include pottery, in particular the tiny cups for serving *qishr*, jars, urns and vases of all sizes. There are plenty of brilliantly hued hand-woven and dyed fabrics available, including shawls. Some of the Yemeni embroidery is superb. Look out, too, for the fragrant spices, perfumes and small boxes of incense, but don't forget the little earthenware stand needed for burning it. Of interest to philatelists are the first-day covers available at post offices. If you should be tempted to purchase any of the old fire-arms that were imported from western Europe during the Ottoman occupation—and there are plenty of them still around—keep in mind that it is against Yemeni law to export anything over 40 years old without official permission.

Aden was once again declared a free port in May 1991, and tax-free shops are to be found in the Tawahi area.

A little bulky for tourists to transport, but what storage capacity!

Practical Information

Banks. Open from 7.30, 8 or 9 a.m. until noon or 12.30 p.m., depending on region.

Behaviour. Visitors will want to respect the customs of the country by not wearing shorts, sleeveless shirts or short skirts. A woman's direct gaze or smile at a local man could be misinterpreted and should be avoided.

During the holy month of Ramadan Muslims fast and refrain from smoking between sunrise and sunset. Tourists should be considerate and not eat, drink and smoke in public. Dates of Ramadan change yearly.

Climate. There are several distinct climatic regions in the country. The southern and Red Sea coasts (including Aden, Mukalla and Hodeidah) lie in an arid, hot zone. Sanaa, in the central highlands, enjoys milder temperatures (maximum 25–30 °C year-round, minimum 0 °C January and 10 °C July), with rainy seasons in March/April and August. A general rule everywhere is to wear loose, cool clothing, hat and sunglasses.

Credit Cards. Generally accepted only in large hotels, and even then not all types are recognized.

Currency. Since unification, the Yemen has two currencies, the *dinar* (divided into 20 *dirhams*—also called shillings—or 1,000 *fils*), which will eventually be phased out, and the *rial* (divided into 100 *fils*).

For *rials*, the minimum pricing unit is 1 *rial*. (Coins of 25, 50 and 100 *fils* are slowly being removed from circulation.) Banknotes run from 1 to 100 *rials*.

For the *dinar*, the most commonly encountered coins are 50, 100 and 250 *fils*. Banknotes come in 250 and 500 *fils* and 1, 5 and 10 *dinars*.

Health Precautions. Drink bottled water, and bring along salt tablets.

Holidays. May 1 and 22, Sept. 26, Oct. 14, and Nov. 30. If a holiday falls on a Wednesday or a Sunday, most stores will be closed for a long weekend (from Wed. to Fri. or Fri. to Sun.).

Language. Arabic. English is generally understood in large towns.

Post Offices. Open 8 or 9 a.m. to noon or 1 p.m. Saturday to Thursday. In the north, they open also from 4 to 8 p.m.

Taxis. It is advised to negotiate the price of your ride *in advance*.

Tipping. Virtually unknown. Service is included in restaurant and hotel charges.

Photos: Monique Jacot; p.108 Bernard Joliat